Ten Point Plan
For College Acceptance

Ten Point Plan For College Acceptance

By Lawrence Graham

A PERIGEE BOOK

Perigee Books
are published by
G. P. Putnam's Sons
200 Madison Avenue
New York, New York 10016

Cover and Book Design: Tim Metevier
Art Assistant: Deborah Froelich
Illustrations: Herman Costa
Cover Photo: John W.H. Simpson

Library of Congress Catalog Card Number: 81-50610
ISBN 0-399-50678-0
First Perigee Printing, 1982
Second Impression
Printed in the United States of America

To my father, Richard;
my mother, Betty;
and my brother, Richard.

For listening and sharing.

Contents

Foreword

Life is a unique challenge which each of us must structure and develop in order to realize our individual goals. This is no easy task. You cannot purchase fulfillment at the market, nor can anyone hand it to you. It is a soul-searching process that means understanding who you are and what you would like to be. One key to gaining proper insight is formal training, or acquired knowledge through educational pursuits.

In our society, college is one of the paths to accumulated wisdom or knowledge. If you have decided that it is the path for you, then the *Ten Point Plan for College Acceptance* is an invaluable tool in your preparation for admission into the college of your choice.

College is not a fairyland filled with professorial ghouls and gremlins waiting to devour the unsuspecting beginner. It is a minicommunity within the larger community, where you will experience intellectual growth and personal satisfaction. To succeed in the college of your choice, you must select one that has an environment that will stimulate your interests, arouse new curiosities, and motivate you to achieve. This guide gives you a ten point plan for determining the college that will best suit your academic, social, and personal interests; and having made those determinations, it gives you a step-by-step procedure for college acceptance.

Lawrence Graham has developed a very realistic plan for college admission. This is a concise, entertaining, and thought-provoking approach for making a college selection. It is by no means the only method for preparing for college, but it is guaranteed to stimulate your own ideas. It also covers every aspect of the application process. Another unique aspect of this book is that the author wrote it as a college student (he began writing it during his freshman year and it was published during his sophomore year), and the freshness of his college entrance experience shines throughout the book. Mr. Graham intertwines his experiences and those of many other students and parents in each of his ten points. He tells you how it really is, not how it's supposed to be. The greatest attribute this guide affords the reader is a method for doing "your own thing" while still achieving all that one can.

Minnie H. Reed M.A., M.Ed.
Director, Princeton University Career Services

Preface

Confusion, doubt, fright, and anxiety. These are the four evils that plague thousands of college applicants each year as they brace themselves for the long college application process. All these problems are easily avoided if one formulates a College Admissions Plan. The ten simple rules in this book will guide your plan and should put you into the college of your choice, while eliminating all the pain and worry. As one who just recently experienced the process, I know the secrets of survival.

When I began writing this book I had just been accepted into several colleges and universities, so I did not have to turn the clock back twenty or thirty years to remember what the college admissions process was like. I had also taken copious notes during the admissions process, including those subtle but important hints.

The information in these pages, however, comes not only from my experiences. It was compiled through interviews with high school students, college students, parents of students, high school guidance counselors, and college admissions officers. Much of the anecdotal material is taken from actual histories. In other words, you'll be reading about student-interviewer conversations that really took place.

Because colleges in different parts of the country use different methods for selecting and interviewing student applicants, I interviewed at colleges in various areas. All of this was to present you with a better idea of what you're really in for and how to deal with it.

The most important thing to remember while reading this book is that it makes no attempt to preach to you. It only intends to *show* you techniques that have worked for others and that could possibly work for you. Don't feel rushed or nervous while you follow the suggestions that are outlined. On the other hand, don't procrastinate. Putting things off to the last minute will certainly throw you off track and hurt your chances for the college you want. If you feel you're behind schedule, turn to Rule Ten: The No-Procrastination College Calendar and put yourself at the point where you're sure to win this game.

With each rule, you can win another point. Right now, you're just ten points away from college acceptance.

Before I continue, I must express my thanks for all those who aided me in the creation of this book and the information herein. I wish to thank my father, Richard Graham, my brother, Richard, and my uncle, Searcy. Thanks goes to Susan Zeckendorf, my friend and agent, who believed in me and my work. So much goes to my editors, Jim Charlton and Ruth Flaxman, who helped me shape my ideas. Support from the beginning came from Dorothy D. Holloway; Christopher P. Fearon; Harry Jefferson; Jim Merrit; Cynthia Reynolds; Hilarie Cohen; the staff of Sarah R. Weddington, Assistant to the President of the United States; Myles Jackson; Damon Keith; James Wickenden; Mirian Gilbert; Anita Jackson; Leslie Nicholson; Frank Tooni; Martha Homma; Tim Metevier; Dr. Aaron Dolinsky; Dr. Leonard Spearman; Arthur P. Antin; Henry and Cecelia Drewry; Joseph Bickford; Pat Loud; Barbara Binswanger; David Schwartzbaum; Nell Bassett; and the members of the White Plains schools and Princeton University and all those high school and college students that I interviewed.

Thanks to all those parents, counselors, and admissions officers who asked to remain anonymous. Thanks for sharing with me that which you had experienced yourself.

My greatest appreciation is for my mother, Betty, who gave more than I could ever ask for, as she listened, guided, and supported me in my desire to write this book.

Lawrence Graham
White Plains, New York
April 1981

Rule One: Lining Up a College Career

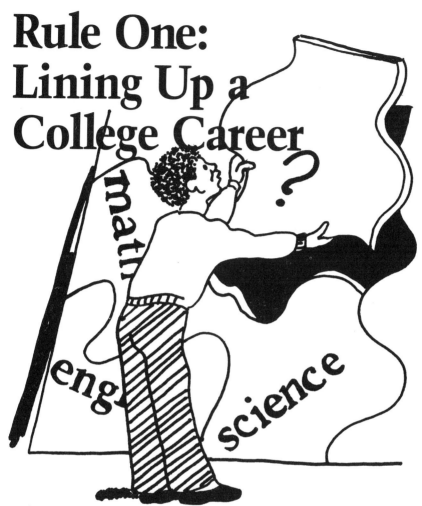

Welcome to the first of the ten simple rules on college admissions. You've already made a big step in your college career by choosing to read this book so give yourself a pat on the back. You certainly could have spent your time watching television, going to the movies, or even listening to the stereo. Why on Earth did you choose to ponder over your college plans? Whatever your reasons are, they have led you in the right direction. Although a college career isn't a person's sole concern in life, it certainly deserves a great deal of time and consideration.

If your older friends or brothers and sisters suffered through the hours of reading, writing, typing, and mailing college applications, pity them. Pity them because they had good reason to suffer. Pity them because they didn't know a better way to organize themselves. Pity them because they didn't have a book of strategies for every step of the

1

admissions process. Pity them because they had to learn by trial and error and because they were misled by confusing admissions statistics and sophisticated language. Feel sorry for them most of all because there was no book like *Ten Point Plan for College Acceptance* to guide them step-by-step through the process. *You* don't have these excuses. Right in front of you is the *inside scoop* on college admissions, so use it to your advantage. Don't let a single strategy or piece of advice slip by you while you're reading this book.

In this book is what an admissions officer would *want* to tell you if he wasn't afraid of losing his job. *Ten Point Plan* tells it all—but in a way you can understand. Rest assured that there are no complicated statistics and graphs in these pages. There is only hard-core information and strategy. This book gets right to the point in a clear-cut, almost entertaining format that lightens the tension of the college application process.

Who Should Read This Book?

Well, if you've read this far, you're probably a high school student or a college transfer student, a parent, a guidance counselor, an admissions officer, or a librarian trying to pass some time in the stacks. No matter who you are, this book can help you in dozens of ways.

For the student, *Ten Point Plan* provides a clear and easy-to-understand guide of what to do, how to do it, and when to do it. Students anywhere from the ninth grade to the second-year college transfer will benefit from the strategies outlined here. The book reveals tried-and-true techniques, which worked for real students. It shows the proper steps for filling out applications, the best way to get recommendations, and the secret of saving time on long essays. Most of all, the student can finally see what the admission officers are looking for, how they interview, and how they select or reject.

For the parent, *Ten Point Plan* supplies a warehouse of resources for financial aid, scholarships, and grants. Paying for college doesn't have to mean six years of winters without heat or months of meatless dinners. Untapped foundations and scholarship search groups exist throughout the country. Many are listed in this book. Also outlined are ways that parents and students can work together. The parent can learn when the child needs help and when he doesn't. Since there is sometimes tension between student and parent over college plans, this book shows how to transform that tension into creating happy parents, successful students, and college acceptance.

For the guidance counselor, *Ten Point Plan* shows how to coordinate the student's best high school curriculum. Counselors can be brought up to date on what the colleges prefer in their student applicants. Those counselors who want to seem as if they have all the answers can read this book and keep it hidden in their desk drawers. For the counselor who wants to suggest the schools to which a student should apply, *Ten Point Plan* can show which schools are in the student's range and which aren't.

For the admissions officer, *Ten Point Plan* proves that the once-hidden secrets on getting into college are no longer hidden—so it will take another twenty years to conceal the facts. Believe it or not, many admission interviewers are nervous about their jobs. Reading about many actual officer-student interviews in this book will relax interviewers and students in almost any situation.

For that librarian in the stacks, *Ten Point Plan* is an entertaining and educational guide to hand to students when they march up to the reference desk and ask about applying to college.

How This Book Is Organized

You've probably noticed that this book isn't composed of chapters—it's made up of "rules." Since college admissions is only a game, there are rules to help you call the shots. The ten helpful rules in this book break up the process so that a student can take everything one step at a time. This book includes a collection of financial-aid sources and a bibliography of books that can aid students in special circumstances. Most beneficial is the "college preparation calendar," which tells you at a glance when to do what.

The *Ten Point Plan for College Acceptance* is an alternative if you don't have another "in" to your favorite college's admissions office. Even if you have a good school in mind that isn't a top name, you should do all that you can to be sure you're in. This book gives you the full scope of your possible strategies for applying. The other guides merely communicate facts, whereas this one will provide you with the subtleties and options that are available to you. Other guides treat all students as if they were "straight A, 750-SAT-scoring whiz kids." This book recognizes *all* students—the below average, the average, *and* the whiz kids.

What it tells you to do in order to "get in" isn't new. Ambitious and successful students have utilized these strategies for years; they haven't written about it.

But Why Even Go to College?

Many of us arrive at the decision to attend college because of parental expectations, because of counselor pressures, or just because everyone else is doing it. Believe it or not, there are better reasons for attending college. Although you won't experience all the benefits until you've been accepted, they'll surely last a lifetime.

Looking for Jobs

Nowadays, employers want to see a resume before they see you. The first thing they look for is your level of education. If you don't have a college degree, you can forget it. The world is now filled with people who graduated from Everybody's State College. It's necessary to appear more qualified than your competitors, and a good college can help you.

A good college doesn't necessarily mean you've got to go for the Ivy League. But it also doesn't mean that you should settle for any school because it's inexpensive. After all, you must foresee the future earnings and success you'll gain after graduating from a good school. You'll be able to pay off those bills and loans once you're in the job market.

So what makes the student so desirable to an employer? What allows that graduate to get a foot in the door of a business or firm that is reaching full capacity? What allows him to impress the employer with a resume sporting a big-name college on the second line? What gives him the assurance that he can deal with any person on any level? What gives this student the many contacts, made in four years, the clout to get what he wants when he wants it? It's the fact that the student attended a college.

Is It Just Four More Years of Hard Labor?

Although the time we spend on algebraic equations and reading history seems to drag on forever, these studies allow us to realize our abilities. But why must we realize our abilities? Isn't it good enough just to have them? No. If you're like most, you probably hate homework, classwork, or any other kind of work. The best thing about college is that it gives you the opportunity to see what you like the most or, should we say, what you dislike the least.

A college education is something to fall back on just in case you don't strike oil or win the Irish Sweepstakes. At the very least, a college education is a chance to study as much or as little of whatever you want. Most colleges allow you the freedom to take a little English, a little music, a little geology, and so on. Another great advantage is that there are no more teachers that pace up and down the rows with whip and chair. They use more powerful and subtle weapons to get you to study—the pen and the grade book.

For those of you who are tired of hitting the books every night in high school, it's a lot different in college because you set up your own schedule. If you don't want to schedule classes on Fridays, you don't have to. The college system beats the seven-hour school day in elementary and secondary school—most college students have classes only three hours each day.

Social Benefits of College

Although every college campus isn't always booming with fun and excitement, you will no longer have to borrow the car from Mom and Dad to go to the movies. Movies will be right on campus. This new freedom allows you to make new and closer friends. Many of these people will end up being part of a future network of contacts.

The purpose of this rule was to show you how a college education can be an advantage. This rule also served as an introduction to a book that blows the cover off college admissions. While removing the ghastly seriousness from the process, *Ten Point Plan for College Acceptance* presents a college admissions plan that will help you succeed. So go ahead and take command of your future.

Rule Two: Lining Up the Right High School Curriculum

Many students ask if there is a "secret recipe" of courses to follow for ideal college preparation. Although they don't always say it, they're also wondering if there are courses that make them especially marketable to colleges. They use the word *marketable* because they've heard that you have to sell your soul for college acceptance. The truth is that you merely have to present an *honest but favorable impression* of yourself.

First of all, there is no one "secret recipe" of courses—there are many. While you use these recipes, it's important to realize that they will not only make you more presentable (or marketable) but will also make you better prepared for the more rigorous college curriculum. The time to start thinking about the right courses is as soon as possible. Don't wait until the semester before you're accepted or rejected by the college of your choice. College admissions officers are trained to identify the student who took Basket Weaving and Finger Painting throughout high school until that last semester of advanced physics, honors history, calculus, and Spanish 2.

High Grades and Easy Courses vs. Low Grades and Hard Courses

The Student's View

In his sophomore year at high school, Frank's parents warned him that in order to get into college, he would have to get as many A's as possible. To Frank, this seemed impossible, since he found his courses such a challenge. He realized that he would have to take easier courses in order to receive higher grades. Once Frank had switched each course to its equivalent on a lower level, he found himself in classes that either were too slow for him or were teaching work that he had already learned. He thought this was great because he could now cut down on the time he spent studying and still bring home the grades that colleges want.

The College View

College admissions officers want more from a student than good grades. They want to see a wide range of challenging courses. Of course it's great to get a high grade-point average, but colleges look for those students who also display high academic promise. That promise includes the desire to study and learn new and difficult ideas. Looking at Frank's records, we see good grades, but we don't know his potential. We know how he works when the work load is demanding. The student who refuses to challenge himself will also be refusing a college acceptance.

The Student's View

At the other end of the spectrum, we have June. A senior now, she's been called Bookworm June for the past three years because she takes only advanced courses. Although her grades remained at the level of C, June kept signing up for the accelerated curriculum. June liked the challenge of hard courses, and it pleased her even more to know that colleges look for students who take challenging courses.

The College View

What June didn't realize is that colleges want students who are realistic about their strengths. While June worked and studied every minute of the day, she kept a poor record on exams and assignments. College admissions officers are looking for mature students who recognize the difference between realistic and unrealistic goals. A college would be afraid to accept June because she is inclined to overload herself to the level of failing.

The Student's View

Clara was an average student in all her courses except math. Throughout grammar school she had loved and excelled in math classes. When it came time for high school, Clara enrolled in the advanced math program. She was able to maintain a B average in all of her classes, but she felt odd that most of the advanced math students were also in advanced English and history as well. Her counselor advised her to remain in regular English and history unless it became too easy. Clara did what was recommended; she also continued to excel in advanced math. When she applied to college, she was viewed as an advanced student.

The College View

Too many students feel that if they are in one advanced class, they should be in all advanced courses. One does not have to be accelerated in every subject in order to qualify as an advanced student. Colleges recognize a student's strengths by seeing how they perform in a particular situation. They are impressed by the student who realizes his strength and tries to build on it. Colleges are not impressed by the student who thinks he is an honors history student just because he is an honors math student.

Avoiding Your Weakness vs. Concentrating on Your Strength

This subheading probably seems repetitive, but once you see what Charlie and Kevin did, you'll notice a big difference between the two.

The Student's View

Charlie was a sophomore in a two-year college. He was ready to transfer to a four-year, fairly selective university. Fortunately, Charlie had fantastic grades throughout high school and in the semesters at college. Charlie had one weakness that he shouldn't have ignored. He was a terrible math student. He would panic at the simplest equation and refuse to try to work it out if he wasn't forced to. In the tenth grade, his high school no longer insisted that he take math. Naturally, Charlie dropped out of math for the remaining years in high school. When he began two-year college, he avoided any courses requiring a knowledge of math. After applying to several four-year colleges, he was rejected by all except two, which he was afraid to attend—they both required two semesters of calculus.

The College View

Charlie was a good student in the courses he took, but he was not motivated to learn that which challenged him. The colleges rejected him because he was not a well-rounded person. Although he could write well and learn American and European history, he ignored a major area of education—mathematics. Charlie could skate through high school and two years of junior college without math, but he was not going to succeed in four-year college that way. Those colleges that accepted him are very typical. A college may accept you if you haven't taken a particular subject, but they won't let you graduate from their school until you've taken the subject under their auspices. Keep in mind that most colleges require that you take a certain number of courses in specified subjects whether you've studied them before or not. Make it easier on yourself by taking a little bit of everything in high school so that you can fulfill those college requirements without a struggle.

The Student's View

Kevin was similar to Charlie except that Kevin took the easier way out by simply concentrating on his strength. His strength happened to be in French and Spanish. Kevin was also in his second year at a two-year college. He was sure he would be accepted by a good four-year college because he had maintained a B average in all of his courses. But what were his courses? French Grammar, Advanced Spanish Composition, French Literature, Spanish History, and Spanish Literature. Since Kevin's two-year college had no course requirements, he could concentrate on whatever subject he wanted.

The College View

Because Kevin concentrated only on his strengths, he failed to maintain a well-rounded record. Taking courses that allow you to build on your talents is great, but limiting yourself to just your strengths can hurt you, as it did Kevin. He was eventually rejected by all the colleges he applied to because they didn't know if he had any aptitude outside of his language abilities. Unfortunately, many high schools and junior colleges don't require that students take a wide selection of courses. If students don't discipline themselves, often they'll find themselves taking only what they enjoy. If your guidance counselor insists that you take a course in a subject you've never studied, it's wise to give it a try.

The Student's View

Perhaps Julia found the solution to Charlie's and Kevin's problem. Julia had a problem that was very similar to Charlie's. She detested math and tried to avoid it like the plague. But her guidance counselor suggested that she take a semester of math. Julia decided that she would give math a try, but she was sure she wouldn't receive a good grade. Instead of working for the usual grades, Julia planned to take the course pass/fail. She preferred pass/fail because letter-graded courses add too much pressure. Therefore, she was able to work with the confidence that she wouldn't wreck her grade-point average.

The College View

How do the colleges view Julia's record? There are a couple of ways that they could interpret her pass/fail choice. They might think that she wanted to experiment in math to see if she liked it, or they might think that math was just as easy for her as history or science. After all, the colleges don't know how well you score in a course unless you take it letter-graded. The pass/fail option tells only whether you passed or failed. In other words, the colleges didn't know if Julia received an A-plus or a D-minus in her math course. Many high schools and junior colleges offer the pass/fail grading option. Make use of it if it removes the pressures of taking a course you'd be afraid to take, but only use it in emergencies.

Foreign Languages: A Necessity

Yes, you have to take a foreign language to get into college. If you think that's bad, it's recommended that you study a language for at least three years. It's not as dreadful as it sounds because language classes will be a welcome relief from those college courses that give pages and pages of reading assignments. Colleges feel that a foreign language allows you to learn more about a foreign culture. Although this is one of the greatest benefits of learning a foreign language, it's hard to tell a tenth grader (who hates conjugating the past tense) that before long he will be able to converse with Europeans. Even if you never learn to speak the language with a proper accent, you may be able to use it for your college essay. A college essay written in Latin would certainly shock the admissions officers.

If you're still not convinced that a foreign language is useful, just wait until you've started college. Most schools require that you take two semesters of a language, whether you've studied it before or not. You'll find that learning a new language in college is twice as hard as learning it in high school. So get a jump on them now.

What Other Courses Are Necessary?

Unfortunately, colleges aren't impressed if you took four years of high school physical education. In addition to those *three years of a foreign language,* they expect to see *four years of English.* This is a requirement you better not avoid because English is the root to understanding almost everything. If you mix some creative writing with the grammar courses, it will make it easier for you. If your school offers journalism, that also counts as English. *Two or three years of history* is recommended, as well as *two or three years of a science* (excluding psychology). Whether you are in accelerated math or not, you should, *at least, take algebra, geometry, and pre-calculus.* Although it's not required, calculus is recommended too. It's a good idea to take some electives like music, psychology, sculpture, or other courses that allow you to use your imagination or talents in a creative way. All of these recommendations probably sound like what your guidance counselor has been telling you. There's no doubt that you think you don't need to learn so much history, math, etc. You're probably right. You probably have learned all that you will ever use, but remember who's calling the shots—the colleges. They don't care how well you write or how much you know—you just better have had those four years of English. Even if that fourth year taught you absolutely nothing, it better be on your record. So please them—it's really not that painful.

Another course that you should take (but which isn't required) is high school typing. A semester in a typing class is extremely helpful because research papers are frequent in college, and you'll be up all night if you use the hunt-and-peck typing method. If you can't fit a typing class into your schedule, enroll in a night course or practice at home. Unless you can afford the cost of a hired secretary, it will be worthwhile learning to type your own work.

That's about all you'll need to fill the basic course requirements. Of course it seems like a lot, but the work you get in college will basically be an accelerated version of high school courses. So learn the basics before you get hit with the heavy stuff.

Courses for Summer Study

You might ask what possesses one to voluntarily attend a school during the summer. It's actually a great idea if you really want to see what college is like. In most cases, you will enroll with a course load similar to that of a college freshman. You would also have the opportunity to live in a college dormitory and see what campus life is like. These summer college programs are basically for high school juniors and seniors. It really doesn't matter which college you choose for your summer study.

You can still reap some of the benefits of summer college courses if you are just a day student two or three times a week. These courses can give you a good background for the harder work you'll be facing. In addition, the admissions officers are impressed by a student who has the motivation to learn in the summer too. Many students will use these summer courses to brush up on their weaknesses. If you've done consistently poor work in high school history, try a short summer course in history. If you do well, you can send the grade to the colleges when you apply. If you don't do well, you don't have to tell anyone. Some colleges will even allow you to transfer the summer credits to your final college record.

Ask your guidance counselor about these programs. They're offered throughout the country by good boarding schools and colleges. The basic requirement for you to enroll in the programs is for you to be enrolled in an accredited high school.

Using Advanced Placement Courses

Many colleges give credit to students for their work in high school advanced placement courses. If you are especially strong in a particular subject, see if your high school has an advanced placement course or allows independent study to prepare for the advanced placement (AP) exam. These exams are given in the spring of each year. If you score well on these exams, your college may grant you a semester of credit for that subject. Students who score well on several AP exams are frequently allowed to skip the freshman year and enroll as college sophomores.

Taking the College Board Exams

A major part of your high school curriculum is your exams. During your senior year you'll be hearing so much about the College Boards, you'll start to believe they're a group of omniscient gods that follow you night and day. The first exam you will be taking that is in anyway affiliated with college admissions is the Preliminary Scholastic Aptitude Test (PSAT). It'll seem as though they're trying to spring the test on you, so expect it within the first two months of your junior year. This test is not optional, and they say that it's best not to study for it. Take some advice and study by reviewing your ninth- and tenth-grade math.

Although the PSAT is composed of a verbal section and a math section, it's difficult to review for the verbal section on short notice. Most counselors will tell you not to study because the PSAT is just a practice exam. The PSAT is not just practice for the Scholastic Aptitude Test (SAT). Actually, a high PSAT score will enable you to become a scholarship winner in the Merit Program or in the National Achievement Scholarship Program for Outstanding Negro Students.

Taking Achievement Tests

In addition to the PSAT, you'll have to take at least three one-hour exams called achievement tests. These exams test your knowledge in specific subjects, such as biology, French, English composition, American history, etc. The highest score is 800 points. It's up to you which ones you will take, but it's good to take the ones that you have recently studied in a high school course. In other words, if you take a chemistry course in the junior year, take the chemistry achievement test in June of that year. If possible, take one achievement test at the end of sophomore year so that you don't have to take all three at once.

You have a better chance to prepare for these tests since many guides are published that feature sample test questions. Barron's educational guides can prepare you for achievement tests in English, American and European history, the foreign languages, the sciences, and two levels of mathematics. If you want to try a test but aren't sure you will do well, you can always cancel the scores at the conclusion of the test. Many students do this, and that test score never shows up on test records (even if you try the entire exam).

Unfortunately for the testing service, the administration of the achievement test has a flaw in it. This flaw, however, can work in your favor if you follow the steps Judy laid out. In Judy's sophomore year in high school she took advantage of the option to cancel her score. She took the math and English tests in June of the sophomore year. She immediately cancelled the English score. The following December she took the English again, along with the French exam. This time she also canceled the English score after taking the exam. By June of junior year, Judy felt she had had enough practice on the English achievement test to take it again and allow the scores to be reported. There's an example of using the system to one's advantage. You don't have to do this if you don't feel it's necessary. After all, you don't need help to score well on these college board exams, do you?

The Two Biggies: The SAT and the ACT

The most popular abbreviation you'll hear during the entire admissions process is SAT. It stands for Scholastic Aptitude Test and can also mean Suspense and Terror if you let it take you by surprise. Most colleges expect applicants to have taken the SAT or the American College Test (ACT) during junior year or the fall of the senior year. By all means, review for the one you plan to take. Most colleges ask only for the SAT, but check with your counselor to make sure. The SAT tests verbal and math aptitude. The maximum for each part is 800. The average verbal SAT score is about 430 and the average math SAT is 465. Don't fear, though, because you get an instant 200 points for writing your name. Since you will *lose* credit for wrong answers on the SAT, random guessing will hurt you. The maximum for the ACT is 36 points.

There are books, manuals, and courses that prepare you for the SAT. Don't hesitate to get any help you can. Find out when you can register during your junior year. If you are not pleased with the first set of scores, you can retake the test in the fall of senior year. This is still enough time to send the scores to your colleges. Most students scores increase when they take the SAT a second time. Your scores are sent to your home a few weeks after the exam.

With your tests and high school courses all lined up, you can start thinking about where you can apply. Rule Three will show you a simple way to select the colleges that will be right for you.

Rule Three: Deciding on the Right Team

Before you read any further, take a deep breath and tell yourself that before this college ordeal is over, you'll probably get a rejection or two. But believe it or not, you can still go to the college of your choice. If you've followed this logic, you're probably wondering how you can be rejected *and* attend the college of your choice. The simple solution is to have a few choice schools. That's why this third rule is so essential. We've got to learn how to choose the schools that are right for us. Each school we apply to should be a school we would be proud to attend. Like the rest of this book, this rule will benefit you if you're applying to college for the first time or if you are already in college but want to transfer to another one.

Although choosing the right schools is sometimes sticky, there are a lot of tricks that help uncover a school's façade. This rule will show you how to get the inside scoop on every aspect of college—what to look for when it's time to apply.

Choosing a few colleges that satisfy your needs does not have to be difficult. The best way to begin is to get hold of a general listing of every college in the country. This is the time when those large, catalog-type reference guides on colleges can be helpful. Drop by your high school or public library reference section and take out the Barron's Profiles of American Colleges or *Lovejoy's College Guide*.

It's crazy to buy these expensive books because every library has them, and you'll probably need only about twenty-five out of the nearly one thousand pages. These colossal catalogs are helpful because they provide about four paragraphs of general information on each school. Although they don't give you any inside information, they do give you the location, size, sex ratio, admission requirements, and tuition of each school.

Within the first few pages of Barron's, you'll find a listing of colleges (grouped according to their level of competition for admission). This listing has divided the colleges into six categories: (1) most competitive (GPA B+, SAT 650); (2) highly competitive (GPA B, SAT 600); (3) very competitive (GPA B−, SAT 550); (4) competitive GPA C, SAT 500); (5) less competitive; and (6) noncompetitive. This constant use of the word *competitive* means absolutely nothing to the bewildered student until he or she reads the Grade Point Average (GPA) and Scholastic Aptitude Test (SAT) score distribution for each of the "competitive" categories. For example, according to Barron's, a college listed in the competitive category would usually accept students with a GPA C and above and SAT scores of at least 500. The other divisions of competition are explained in a similar manner. You'll find that these catalogs constantly report exact scores and grades like 650 or 500 or B+ or C. Remember that these are only "mean figures" that represent a type of midpoint. So if a school's mean SAT is 600, they may very well accept scores 200 points above or below 600. A mean is just to give you a rough idea of the middle range.

How High to Shoot

The most important thing to remember while using this chart is that the breakdown is a very rough estimate of each school's level of competition. Just because your grades are all B, don't think that you won't get into the most competitive schools. Remember that each school is looking for something different in each applicant. Certain schools might ignore your low grades and low scores because of your special talents in music, athletics, or drama. These guides, however, can be harmful to the student who follows them too closely. Unfortunately, there are many students who will overlook colleges that are above their range of scores—that is a mistake. The guides *only provide averages and estimates.* Don't be afraid to select a few schools above your category of competition. After all, there are many students accepted by the Ivy League each year who have received SAT scores as low as 450.

Factors to Consider

As you read on, try to decide what type of school is best for you. Keep in mind that although you'll be applying to about six or seven colleges, each one has to be *carefully* selected. It's worth taking your time since you'll be spending four years at one of them. It's not time yet to jump out and visit the colleges. You first have to decide what you want in a school, and to do this, you must consider many aspects of each college. The rest of this rule will show you how and what to consider.

Course Offerings

One of the factors to consider when choosing the right colleges to apply to is the selection of courses. If you want to be a chemistry major and then a biochemist, a fine arts college with no science courses will do you no good. Many students don't realize this, but the same subjects are not offered at every school. If you must take engineering courses, find out if all of your colleges offer them.

Location of the College

A primary consideration is the school's location. The location can be further described by (1) distance and (2) setting. Many of us decide in high school that the best way to escape from our parents is by choosing a college completely across the globe. And then there are many of us who want to be near home and family. Naturally, there are benefits and drawbacks to both choices. It might be good to get away from dominating parents who refuse to allow you any independence. But remember that when you gain independence, you also gain more responsibility—so don't plan on your parents washing your clothes or returning your overdue library books when you're in Oregon and they're in Florida. Additional drawbacks to being far away from home are the costs of transporting yourself and all your "junk" to your dormitory room. Since there are always a few long vacations during each semester, you're traveling not just at the beginning and end of the school year. Spending two weks on an empty campus just because you're too far to make the trip home can be pretty lonely and depressing.

Being close to home will mean cheaper phone bills, but it may not teach you to be an independent person if you run back home each weekend. When they are too close to home, many students refuse to take part in the social life and the campus activities. So before finally deciding on the distance of the school, do some thinking about transportation costs. Also examine the pros and cons of having Mom and Dad around the corner or across the map. Now you're ready to choose the proper setting. As we consider different settings, we will look at two extremes—the city campus and the rural campus.

The City School. There are college dormitories and classroom buildings set in the middle of bustling, smog-filled cities or on acres of a grassy country club campus. Each type offers something entirely different. City schools are usually surrounded by old neighborhoods that are havens of street crime. A city school is also likely to run out of dormitory space sooner than a campus school. The nuisance is even greater when you've got to use a subway or bus to get from class to class or class to dorm. Although you'll never find a dull moment in the fast-paced city streets and its movies, bars, stores, and restaurants, you'll be missing the togetherness that a secluded "rah-rah" campus college produces.

The Campus School. The campus school in a secluded rural area is great for the student who can't afford to be distracted by the busy city. It also allows students to get to know one another better, since there's nowhere to escape. Unlike the city, the main problem here may be the boredom that is created by a dreary country town that hardly merits a position on the map. You will often find these to be "suitcase schools" that almost die on the weekends because everyone escapes to the nearest city each Friday night.

Cost of the School

When looking at the cost of a college, it's essential that you still apply even if your parent's can't afford the tuition. The most expensive colleges have already hit ten thousand dollars. At these schools and less expensive schools, a large percentage of the students are given special financial scholarships.

Don't panic if you don't think you'll get a scholarship. If a college accepts you and you've explained your financial need, they'll make it so you *can* afford the cost. (For more information, see Rule Nine on Financial Aid and the Financial Aid Appendix.)

Aspects of the Smaller Colleges

The next factor to consider when selecting colleges is the size of the student body. A four-year college's student body may range between

750 and 30,000 students. In other words, you can be anything from a personality to an ID number simply by selecting a certain size school. As we examine small and large schools, keep in mind that we are examining extremes (i.e., the smallest and largest schools) and their advantages and disadvantages.

There's much to be said for small schools if you fit in—you'll immediately have a sense of belonging. You'll find that teachers will evaluate *you* as an individual instead of a student ID number. Many small schools have smaller classes. This means that you not only get more individualized instruction but become more acquainted with the professor. It might not seem important now, but when you're nearing an F for the final grade, a good rapport with the teacher can only help. This is not to say that you can just raise your grades by dating or partying with the teacher. This, of course, means that borderline failures are in a better position if they have a one-to-one relationship with the teacher.

Naturally, there's a bad side to everything. On the *social scene,* the adantages of the smaller schools (750 to 2,500 students) are fantastic as long as you walk, talk, eat, look, study, and dress like everyone else. In other words, you've got a better chance of surviving if you are a conformist. This is not to say that you can never do your own thing. But on the whole, individuality in the social arena is not as accepted in the smaller colleges. Since the school is so small, everyone sees and hears your every motion. When you don't mix, you can easily become the oddball. Most small colleges boast about the intimacy that exists in their school, which is a frightening but honest fact—if you're not accepted by a particular clique, the only existing intimacy is between teacher and student. If you are still insisting on the smaller schools, you are guaranteed to find more interaction among people. More interaction can mean closer relationships. Whatever you decide, make sure you realize that you'll be living with the same group for four years.

Extracurriculars in the Small College. The variety of extracurricular activities is often limited in the smaller schools because there are fewer people to take part in various sports or activities. Although most students will be satisfied with the available organizations on campus, make sure that they offer what *you* want. Don't assume that every college has a debate team or a soccer team. Some of the major activities may not exist at the very small colleges because of a lack of funds or a lack of participants.

Last but not least, we want to examine what you've all been waiting for—the *academic curriculum* in the small school. Since very small schools can't offer the widest choice of courses, you must make sure that your choice of schools will offer a wide range of subjects. Most of us don't know what our major area of study will be, so we need to study a little of everything. Keep in mind that the best schools will give you a variety of courses. Even if you don't think you'll ever major in psychocryptographics or computeranthromathology, isn't it good to know that it's there if you want it. On a more serious note, try to choose the school that offers you a wide selection of courses and programs.

If all this has convinced you that the smaller schools are an unnecessary nuisance, don't think that the larger schools are any better. They're all about equal because each size has advantages and disadvantages. Different people want different things from a school. You must consider the bright side *and* the dark side of various schools. Without a realistic picture of small vs. large colleges, the naïve student can easily be in for four years of hell.

Aspects of the Larger Schools

Now let's look at those outrageously large universities that have as many, or more than, 25,000 students. Many of us were born in towns with fewer than 25,000 people and just can't adjust to a congestion this great. On the whole, you can say good-bye to the individualized classroom attention and hello to the colossal lecture halls. To many of us, the large school offers an opportunity to seize anonymity. We can sit in the lecture and never be noticed by the professor—or better yet, we can *not* sit in the lecture hall and never be noticed. These larger schools really can't discipline the student who doesn't attend class because there's no one to keep tabs on the daily attendance.

Socially, the introverts, extroverts, and perverts have a better chance in the larger school. They can fall into the crowd. Their little problems can find hiding places, or they can find other students who will tolerate all sorts of bad habits. Although they are no big happy family, the big schools do offer someone or something for everyone. Remember that family-type unity doesn't exist, so everyone basically does his own thing. This frequently leads to greater individuality and sometimes to eccentricity or the "college freak." The "college freak" is a student who realizes that he can do anything and everything and get away with it because the school is too large and disorganized to discipline him. If you have an absolutely repulsive personality, you can easily move from person to person and never worry about running completely out of friends.

When it comes to *extracurricular activities*, the choices are usually wide and exciting in the larger colleges. Since there is usually plenty of money that goes into activities and clubs, there will probably be something for you. The biggest disadvantage seems to be team sports. The problem here is that there is just too much competition to get on the teams. From football to gymnastics to crew, you'll sometimes find twenty-five students competing for one open position. This lessens your chances but increases the excitement if you survive the competition. In the large schools the variety of organizations will always give you a chance to meet different types of people from different parts of the country.

Sports Recruiting by the Large Universities. By all means, don't be discouraged by the thought of competing in your particular sport at a large university. There are two great benefits that outweigh the fright of competition. They are called team recruitment and sports scholarships. It happens that the large universities are the homes of great sporting teams. In order for these schools to retain a high-quality team, they constantly look for good high school athletes. Recruiting has been a way to bring future professional athletes into the college sports arena and train them for the professional world. Sports recruiters from large colleges visit high schools and high school sporting competitions. Frequently they will write to high school coaches and ask for students' names and sports records. If the college sports recruiter is interested in anyone, he or she will then pay the high school a visit.

If you are interested in a particular university but are afraid no recruiter will discover you, it's time to do some legwork and paperwork. Get to a directory of college addresses and prepare a letter to the coach of the college team in which you are interested. Discuss your sports record, your background, and your interest in continuing sports competition at their university. This is a great way to draw attention to yourself. If the coach wants you, *he or she will help fight your case at the admissions office.* Few people realize this, but many universities set aside several openings for students who are recruited because of their sports records. These people don't necessarily plan on continuing sports past the college level.

Once you're accepted by the college, they may offer you a full or partial sports scholarship. These scholarships frequently cover the entire cost of the tuition. Getting accepted and receiving a scholarship is certainly worth the time it takes to write a note to the team coach. So now you see that large universities have a lot to offer outside the classroom.

Academics at the Large Schools. Now we're back with the *academic curriculum* again. But, with the larger colleges, you have a greater selection of courses, since they usually offer a greater number of course departments. You aren't tied down to the basic three R's of reading, 'riting, and 'rithmetic. You can now choose from and mix every possible subject and get into the new "mode of thought" courses. By mixing course subjects, you can come up with areas of study, such as European Psyhco-Art (psychological studies of European artists) or History of Science (the study of science without all the chemistry, biology, or time-consuming labs). This latest craze is popular in the larger schools that have enough money and students to fill the classes.

This is about all you're going to hear concerning the pros and cons of large and small schools. Remember that the information relates to the largest and smallest schools. Of course all schools cannot simply be categorized as large or small. Don't stop here because there is a lot more to consider before you can choose the right college.

State vs. Private Colleges

You may not realize it, but a college's character has a lot to do with the group that operates it. You can choose any state in the Union and find at least one state-owned or -operated college or university. The purpose of these state-owned schools is to make education more affordable and more accommodating to the state's residents. The greatest drawback to state-owned colleges is that they reserve more than 75 percent of the school for in-state residents. Not only does this make it hard for you to get into another state's schools, but it also limits the variety of people you'll meet. Although the quality of education in these schools is often as good as that in some private colleges, in many cases they lack the prestige that is often helpful when you're job seeking. For some people, the benefits of a lower-priced state school outweigh the advantages from the private school's prestige.

Now it's time for the Private College Rebuttal. These colleges usually brag about their smaller class sizes and their students' varying backgrounds. They can get away with this because their student bodies are composed of students from all over the country (and frequently from around the world). Although the private college's tuition is usually well above that of the state schools, most private schools have more money and can provide more financial aid to students. Unfortunately, there are some cases where students applying for financial aid at private colleges lose out and don't qualify. (See Rule Nine for ways to pay for college.)

Safety Schools

When you choose a group of colleges to apply to, you should include three colleges that you're 90 percent sure you'll get into, considering your grades and scores. This type of school should be selected primarily by its "required" scores and GPA's. In other words, a college is not a "safety" if they are looking for a 500 SAT and you have only a 430 SAT. A safety school should fall *well within* your range of scores and grades. These safety schools should also be ones that you wouldn't mind attending if you are later faced with rejections from other colleges. If you messed up in high school, you don't have to mess up in college, and a safety school is a place where you would be able to retain a high average.

This just about completes the list of factors to consider when choosing colleges. Will it be a small private college far away from home, the large state university in your area, or perhaps something in between? Now that you know some of the things to expect from each type of school, you can select about nineteen or twenty colleges that fit your own requirements. Refer to one of those large guides that we mentioned earlier and take down the colleges' addresses. Remember, it's not yet time to visit any colleges, since we're still working with a preliminary list of colleges. You have a few more things to do before you can eliminate eight or nine schools from your list.

Sending for Application Material

Since it's a little crazy to apply to nineteen or twenty colleges, you'll need more information on each school to further limit your number of applications. You can send away to colleges for their course catalogs, pamphlets, and application forms just about anytime during the year. There's nothing wrong with starting in your junior year or even in your sophomore year. Write to each of the schools on regular 4" x 6" postal cards, giving your return address. You don't need a formal letter or envelope. At this point, a letter and envelope are just a hassle for the secretary. A printed or typed paragraph like the following will suffice:

To the Admissions Office:

My name is Susan Danfield and I am a seventeen-year-old student at West Bay High School. Could you please send me information and an application form for your school.

Thank you very much.

Susan Danfield
133 So. Columbus Avenue
Mount Plains, MO 19823

You can breathe easily for a few weeks until you begin receiving the requested college material. Then you can review the material and check whether they offer the courses, activities, and facilities that appeal to you. Whatever you do, don't take every word as the gospel truth. These pamphlets are designed by advertising professionals who want to sell the school to you.

Since colleges want to attract many students, they'll use photographs, humor, and famous quotations to convince you that their school is the best in the galaxy. Ignore the flowery language and photographs of happy students flocking to and from classes and dining halls. Most students will tell you that the meals and courses will rarely put a smile on your face. Read through all the material and make note of their scholarships and financial-aid information (see Rule Nine).

Visiting the Campus

So now you're ready to hit the road and visit these final eight or nine schools, right? Well, not yet. Trips are expensive, and they are only worthwhile if you know what you're going to be looking for. If the college requires an interview on campus, you really have no choice but to visit the college. (See Rule Five on Interviews.) But if a college doesn't require one, don't ask for one unless you've got some good reasons and good questions to ask when you get there.

It's not essential to visit the schools, but many students do so if (1) they have the time; (2) they can afford the trip; (3) the available information and pamphlets do not answer their questions; or (4) they want to sense the atmosphere themselves. The reasons for not visiting the colleges are as follows: (1) you can always visit them after you've been accepted; (2) you can speak to those alumni who live in your area and ask them questions.

If you are able to afford that visit—go ahead and make it, but plan ahead of time. It's best to visit a campus when the college is in session so that you can get a sense of the classes, activities, social life, etc. Go in the middle of the week. It's best to set aside two days and one night for your visit. This way you have the opportunity to sit in on some classes and lectures.

If you don't know any students at the school, some colleges will provide a student for you to stay with for a couple of days. This is a great idea because a student is one more person who can give you a deeper insight into the college. Ask the student for a tour of the campus, and then sink your teeth right in—and ask, ask, ask! Eat in the dining halls and listen in on conversations. This helps you find out what topics interest these students.

During your visit, stop in at the library after dinner and see if this is a school full of nurds. If everyone is out on the green or at the pub, perhaps this school isn't much of an academic college.

As you walk around campus, you should notice whether the students take pride in their school. Do they throw papers on the ground or write on the buildings? It's also important to take note of the condition of the dormitories, dining facilities, and class buildings. Although many colleges feature near-prehistoric buildings, they should be clean and safe. During your walk, examine the surrounding town, if there is any. Does it appear safe in the evening? Can you spot a five-and-dime store or even a post office?

If you're really brave, you can try a few tactics to see what the students are like socially. Ask them questions. Pretend you're lost and see how friendly and helpful they are. Whatever you do and however you do it, be thorough in your examination. After your visit, you have yourself, your friends, your adviser, and your parents to help you decide which college is best. This is how our next rule, "Wrestling with Your Guidance Counselor and Your Parents," will help you.

Information on Transferring from Two- or Four-Year Colleges

If you're already in a college as a freshman or sophomore and you want to transfer to another school, you will follow the same procedure for selecting schools as was outlined in this rule. The only difference is that you should write to the admissions office and ask for a "transfer admission" application. The school will mail you any material concerning the forwarding of high school grades and scores, as well as the grades from your present college. The process is just as simple as it was when you first applied. But there is a catch. Transfer applicants are usually considered only if they have not spent more than two years at the original college. In other words, if you are a freshman or sophomore, your chances are good. But applying after your sophomore year is taking a big risk.

Other than the application, the procedure for selecting and getting into the right college is the same as it was the first time around.

Rule Four:
Wrestling with
Your Guidance
Counselor and
Your Parents

"I'll stop nagging when you get into Harvard!"

"Orville, make your mother happy—go to Penn and meet a nice girl."

"Look, David, who cares about the social life—it's MIT!"

"I don't care if this is your third SAT—next time you'll break 650 if it kills me!"

"Dear Mr. Admissions Officer, my daughter, Heather, is really a nice girl. She helps around the house and wants to be a nurse. We raised her with the finest manners. Please, please, please let her into your school."

How do you prevent these things from happening? If you don't know what I'm talking about, you're lucky. I'm referring to situations created by those middle-aged creatures we call excessively concerned parents. Their concern seems to cause so much trouble while we're taking college entrance exams, selecting schools, interviewing at colleges, or even waiting for an acceptance letter. *By no means does this refer to all parents. Don't think that your parents are being too pushy because they want you to attend college.* You can, however, assume that they're pushy when they give you a choice between "any school in Cambridge, Massachusetts." This new rule will show you how to deal with *those parents and counselors who cause trouble*, and, believe it or not, it will also show you how parents and counselors can help.

You'll find that during the ordeal of your application process, you might have to wrestle with your counselor and parents over many issues. Try to understand that they're trying to help you, but also realize that *you* are the best judge of which schools you will like best.

Understanding Your Parents' Concerns

Parents are most likely to display their interest in your college career as you enter your junior year in high school. This is when they begin to hear other parents mentioning their kids' PSAT scores. Many of them, not even realizing what "PSAT" stands for, run around ranting and raving, "Oh, yes, and my Diane got an A– and a B+ on her PSAT. She's just doing so much better than everyone else." "Is that all Diane got? My Bartholomew broke 2,000 on both," Both of these parents enjoy bragging about their children. However, neither realizes that the top score on the PSAT is 80 points.

Before you get too far into the inner workings of the college admissions process, you had better realize that your parents will frequently offer suggestions. Try to understand that no matter how much they nag and complain, they only want the best for you.

How Your Parents Feel

Actually, your step toward college education greatly affects your parents. Although parents may display their emotions in different ways, they all feel a sense of loss. This is probably the first time that you will be out from under their roof for any length of time. To you, this might seem a long-awaited vacation, and it might seem that way to them at first. But after they realize that you're no longer going to be living at home, they almost want to turn back the clock.

Parents react in many ways once their realize that their little Suzie or Jerry is leaving home. They may decide to suddenly tighten the discipline in a final hope to prepare you for the outside world. Some parents will demand that you attend a particular school because it's in a safe neighborhood or close to home. If you disagree with their demands or suggestions—don't fight it out. Discuss your disagreements, keeping the attitude that they are concerned for you. It's up to you to prove that you can fend yourself.

Unfortunately, some students use college as a weapon against their parents. They will sometimes settle on a particular college *only* because a parent prefers another college. This is foolish since the student is ultimately hurting his own academic and social life. After all, it's not Mom and Dad who are going to school—it's you. During this emotional process, notice how your parents react to your decisions and try to iron out problems before they seriously damage your family ties.

Parents and College Planning

Let's first look at how some parents react when it's time for college planning.

Jason's father was getting upset because his son displayed no interest in college. He felt that since Jason was now starting the eleventh grade, college planning should be the main topic of conversation. Instead, Jason spoke only about high school, his friends, and his extracurricular activities. His anxious father began to drop subtle hints like "Just think, Jason, in only two years you'll be on your own."

Of course, Jason realized that his father was hinting about his college plans. The best way to handle a parent like this is to meet with your school counselor and outline some preliminary plans for college. Then you should surprise your parents with the information you have researched. This signals them to stop worrying about you and your plans. If you let them continue to drop hints, they'll soon become frustrated by your refusal to pay any attention. When they start giving you hints, let them know that you appreciate their ideas and that you are already making plans with your guidance counselor.

Handling the Parent Who Compares You with Peers

At Karen's house the situation was handled more directly. Her mother would always bring up the subject of college after she had heard other mothers talking about their kids and their favorite colleges. Karen's mother never seemed to show a genuine concern for Karen's future at college. Her only concern was to have an answer for the mothers who asked about Karen's plans. It reached a point where Karen could predict when the subject would be mentioned. Whenever her mother returned from PTA meetings, grocery shopping, or card games, Karen was confronted with remarks like "I understand Selma's little Jodie is visiting Whittier College next month. I'm sure she'll like it." Or "Someone told me that Eddie Fitzgerald received a two-year scholarship to Dartmouth. That's your kind of school, Karen." Or "Did you hear that little Harriet is already getting interviews for schools. She's got such a great head on her shoulders. Only sixteen and she's looking already. Don't you just envy her?"

Karen's mother was about as subtle as a squeaky wheel. She was determined to get her daughter to pick up on these leads. Her mother used the wrong tactics to get Karen interested in college. Although she meant no harm, her constant comparisons of Karen and other students turned Karen further away from the thought of college.

The best way to handle a parent like this is to say, "Mom, I'm glad you're keeping me up on what people are doing because I've really been busy lately. My guidance counselor and I are supposed to get together in a little while and plan my schedule for college application." This is the best technique because this type of parent will never stop hinting and questioning until he or she knows you have a plan of your own. If your mother or father makes constant comparisons between you and other students, don't be offended. Getting upset will only cause you grief during an already high-tension period.

The Parent with a Big Ego

Most parents don't realize it, but sometimes they suggest unnecessary competition and end up destroying a student's perspective on college. Hector's father not only compared him with other students but created an imaginary competition. Daily he asked Hector which students were looking at which colleges. Hector willingly told him about his friends' interests. His father would then ask about the grades and activities of these friends. Before Hector realized what was going on, his father had presented him with a chart listing his school friends, their scores, grades, and activities. This was to be Hector's competition, and Hector was to keep track of what these people did. Most important, Hector was told to "beat them all." This sounds outrageous, but Hector's father was determined that his son stay ahead of his classmates.

As time went on, Hector's father told him to join more activities at school. His father dictated the test scores that Hector had to beat and the grades he had to exceed. Hector thought this method was rather ridiculous, but he was afraid to disobey his father. After a while, Hector started to perceive college as the finish line in a horse race.

Few of us have parents like this, but we can often turn our parents into vicious competitors once we start telling them about our classmates' grades and activities. Some parents feel threatened by the thought that their child is not near the top or coming out first. Since parents already know that colleges look for the top scorers and the best student leaders, you only build anxiety in a parent by telling them that others are scoring a lot better and are participating in more activities. Although it's good to keep your parents aware of your grades and activities, don't go out of your way to show them how many other students are outdoing you. Remember that *you* are the best judge of your abilities. Don't let an ambitious or overanxious parent change you from a student to a racehorse.

The Bribing Parent

Some parents try to give their kids an incentive to study and to plan for college by offering them gifts and rewards. Although it seems harmless, the parent is actually ruining the son or daughter. Bribes and rewards will cause you to lose sight of what you are capable of doing on your own.

Brenda had always been an average student in high school. When her parents started discussing college, Brenda displayed no interest. Her parents tried strict discipline and punishment as methods to get Brenda to start her college planning. Their last resort was to bribe her with small gifts. When her parents asked her to look into the necessary college entrance exams, Brenda paid no attention. They offered her two new skirts if she agreed to keep informed about the necessary examinations.

Although Brenda had outlined the schools that interested her, she hadn't gotten around to asking for applications. Her anxious parents promised her a ticket to a Broadway play if she sent away for all the applications within a week. Suddenly Brenda realized that she could get almost anything she wanted from her parents by merely procrastinating with her college planning. Since her parents didn't catch on to Brenda's scheme, they continued to bribe and reward her for her study habits and school grades. As time went on, Brenda was able to collect a new wardrobe, a late-night curfew, and a larger allowance. When it came time to study for the SAT, Brenda decided that the stakes should be higher—she was determined to win a new car from her parents. Unfortunately for Brenda, her parents refused to bribe her this time. Brenda decided she would get back at them by not preparing for her SAT.

Brenda lost all motivation when she wasn't rewarded. In the end, Brenda hated her parents for not rewarding her, and her parents were angry because she didn't please them after "all they'd given her." Although bribery is about the worst tactic a parent can use, it is used quite frequently. Even if you do want a new bicycle or more privileges from your parents, don't give them the opportunity to bribe or persuade you into better study habits or making college plans. Work by your own motivation.

Now that you have seen the ways in which some parents will act before the application process, you will have to prepare yourself for the parent who later wants to choose your college for you.

Parents Who Want to Choose Your College

As the time to select the colleges comes around, you may notice a different side of your parents. Although they were fairly calm when there was plenty of time to look at colleges, they now impose their ideas on your selection of schools. There's always a parent who swears he knows what he's doing and pushes you for the Ivy League or their alma mater or whatever. When you see this happening, you have to ignore their suggestions because you'll only find yourself in a school you'll hate for four years.

There are a couple of ways to handle the overbearing parent. The best way is to alert your high school counselor so that when asked by your parents why you're not applying to their favorite schools, you can say, "My counselor feels those schools would not be right for me." Most parents accept your decision more easily when you attribute it to a qualified counselor.

Another method is to agree to apply where they want only if they promise to fill out your applications, write your essays, hunt down your recommendations, appear in your absence at the interview, and attend the school for each semester. If this doesn't work, go back to the first method and discuss it with your counselor.

A Parent's Shattered Dream

Parents have dreams, just as you have dreams. Many parents have always imagined their child attending a particular college. The parent who insists on a certain college cannot be called selfish or inconsiderate. Your refusal to agree with the parent can evoke strange responses. A shattered dream can have a great effect on his or her attitude. The parent may want to strike back at you because you're preventing their dreams from coming true. Although these are only dreams, you have to treat them with a sympathetic awareness.

Explain to your parents that you will be most comfortable with your own final decision and that you hope to receive their support. Once parents realize that you are firm but understanding, they'll be willing to reciprocate.

Counselors and College Planning

Dealing with a guidance counselor during this period is a totally different scene from dealing with parents. Very rarely will you find a counselor who beats around the bush when it comes to college planning. Counselors are usually direct in their interest and direct in their apathy. Since counselors have a basic "college calendar" that they follow for their students, they won't start rushing you without a reason. You should realize that when a guidance counselor tells you to think about colleges, it is *not* too early.

Many students complain that their counselors never get off their backs. If this is how you feel, consider yourself lucky. The time to worry is when your counselor doesn't have time to let you know what's going on or doesn't give you suggestions on college planning. Let's take a look at the counselor during the college planning stages.

You Can't Blame Your Counselor

Jack's counselor had organized a college planning seminar for his fifty students. The counselor told all the students about the meeting well in advance. Unfortunately, Jack had a basketball match on the same day as the meeting. His counselor told him to go to the game because the meeting would last only forty-five minutes and he could get the information at another time. This satisfied Jack, and he went to the basketball game. Two months later he received a letter from the school principal, which said that Jack was on academic probation for ten weeks because he had not registered for the school's aptitude tests and had not submitted an essay on his post-high school plans. This took Jack by surprise. He soon found out that the forty-five-minute meeting that he had missed two months before had informed the students of their school's new policy for juniors. Jack immediately put the blame on his counselor because he hadn't insisted that Jack stay for the meeting. He said that it was the guidance counselor's responsibility to track him down and give him the information.

This is a very typical occurrence, especially during the period of college planning. There is always new information that your counselor must give to you, but he won't always make sure that you get it. You'll find yourself in hot water if you wait for the guidance counselor to look for you because important deadlines can pass. If you've been out of school for a few days, drop by your counselor's office to see if you missed anything important.

The Counselor to Worry About

If you feel your counselor isn't being helpful with your college planning, don't think he will improve unless you tell him your concerns. If you are still dissatisfied with your counselor, it might be time to get another counselor's help. One of your biggest problems will be deciding whether your demands of a counselor are reasonable. The following list describes the role of the ideal guidance counselor:

1. A counselor should let you know about important deadlines and upcoming exams.
2. A counselor should be able to supply advice on your future education.
3. A counselor should allow you the opportunity to visit him at least once every three or four weeks.
4. A counselor should offer constructive criticism of your performance.
5. A counselor should be open to your suggestions and opinions.

You're in deep trouble if your counselor fills none of these basic requirements. A counselor who fills none of these five requirements is not working for your benefit, and you had better complain to him or to the principal if necessary.

Helping Counselors Get the Job Done

You'll find that most colleges require a letter of recommendation from your counselor. In addition to the letter, counselors must send in your school transcripts and any other requested material. Since a counselor has many students and since each of these students' colleges have different deadlines, they can easily lose track of these important dates. You can help them remember by compiling all of the important dates and addresses on one sheet of paper. Your counselor will appreciate your extra effort, and you can be more certain that material will be mailed on time.

A Counselor Can Help

A counselor can be a type of sounding board in addition to informing you of his experiences with other students. Since counselors go through the college application process each year with new students, they are a warehouse of information. A counselor can show you cases involving various students from past years. As long as students' names aren't mentioned, you aren't violating anyone's privacy.

When it came time to find out about college admissions, Peter asked his guidance counselor about her experiences with other students who had grades similar to his. She thought of several examples and told him where the students had applied and where they had been accepted. Peter used these examples as a guide for his own plans. He was now able to predict his own success in college admittance with more certainty.

How Parents Can Help

Don't think that because your mother and father aren't college counselors, they can't give you advice. Parents, like counselors, can serve as sounding boards when you are trying to make certain decisions. The best way to set up a sounding board session with your parents is to ask them to listen to you talk for about thirty minutes. Begin by telling them about your interest in various colleges. Go into depth by discussing your career plans, your desire to be near or far, your desire to attend a competitive school, or even your desire to improve your social life. Ask them to give some feedback to your opinions, but explain to them that you are asking for suggestions—not orders.

They'll feel great doing this favor for you because you included them in your decisions. Your parents wil be less inclined to make unfair demands on you about your college planning if you've already asked for their input.

You can now see how parents and counselors can be a great help and a great challenge. It's up to you to learn from them and still make your own decisions. This is a great step in the admissions process, but once you've decided what *you* want, you will be able to win this game.

Rule Five:
How to Impress
the College
Admissions Office

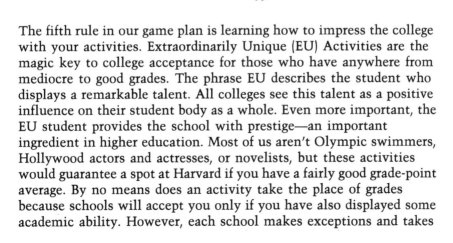

The fifth rule in our game plan is learning how to impress the college with your activities. Extraordinarily Unique (EU) Activities are the magic key to college acceptance for those who have anywhere from mediocre to good grades. The phrase EU describes the student who displays a remarkable talent. All colleges see this talent as a positive influence on their student body as a whole. Even more important, the EU student provides the school with prestige—an important ingredient in higher education. Most of us aren't Olympic swimmers, Hollywood actors and actresses, or novelists, but these activities would guarantee a spot at Harvard if you have a fairly good grade-point average. By no means does an activity take the place of grades because schools will accept you only if you have also displayed some academic ability. However, each school makes exceptions and takes students who might not excel in scholarship but who have done something that is so EU that your admission to their school would be a great asset.

Why Schools Want EU Students

A school's major concerns are prestige and money. Naturally this would be refuted by the deans and professors of those schools who claim that their primary concern is an emphasis on fine education, but look at the schools with the finest education. They all have two things in common: They're prestigious, and they're rich. Evidently, the value of fine education is somehow tied in with the values of prestige and money. A simple example of this would be the Big Three: Harvard, Yale, and Princeton. These are the three most prestigious, richest, and finest educational institutions in the country. It's hard to say which quality is the primary concern. One important fact is that the admissions office determines all three concerns simply through its annual selection of students.

PRESTIGE When a school selects an EU student who has received publicity for a specific talent, such as inventing a computer or running statewide political campaigns, the public begins to associate fine students with that school's name. This gives the school a favorable reputation, or *prestige* . . . which then causes rich families and companies to want to be associated with such a prestigious organization and they give . . .

MONEY to the school in order to have a classroom or building in their name (such as the Rockefeller Library at Brown University, the Rockefeller buildings at University of Chicago, and the Rockefeller-named dormitories at Princeton University). The prestige of the school is gained (or bought) by the rich family as they write the checks—a fair trade. Since good professors and quality facilities are expensive, that money is used to pay for a . . .

FINE EDUCATION This is what establishes or reaffirms the fact that the school is well worth its prestige and rich endowment. This continues the cycle because a fine education is what attracts students and highly qualified professors to the faculty (which justifies charging you a high tuition).

As an outlook of the future, the school sees its EU students graduating to become famous, rich, and intelligent individuals, who will naturally enhance the school's prestigious reputation for producing fine students and increase the endowments as the rich alumni contribute generously during annual giving.

Choosing the Impressive EU Activity

As you read about the following characters, you'll learn how to turn your hobbies into activities that will impress every admissions office. You'll soon see that with a little extra effort, your hobby, sport, or talent will become a key to the college of your choice.

Steve Campus vs. Mr. Incredible

Steve Campus, an average to good high school student, had a great interest in government. He was well liked by all the students and was nominated each year as class representative. He eventually ran for class president in the eleventh year.

Mr. Incredible received the same grades as Steve and also had an interest in government. Instead of limiting his experience to student government, he expanded his goal to include city politics. Therefore, he used the school as his training ground for a future endeavor. He ran for class president of the ninth grade and became active in his area's League of Women Voters. That summer Mister Incredible volunteered for a local city councilman's campaign. By the following summer he had worked with the councilman to such an extent that he met many other city leaders. He then became involved and was finally paid as a campaign worker by his eleventh school year. With student support and newfound knowledge of running campaigns, he ran for the highest position in his high school—president of the school government.

Unfortunately, there are thousands of school presidents applying for admission, but there are only a few who try to make their accomplishments seem impressive. Because Mr. Incredible knew this, he got busy and began to implement a few new programs such as a fund-raiser activity for a popular charity. Colleges love to see benevolent politicians like Mr. Incredible because it makes him appear less of a political "cutthroat." The admissions people look at Mr. Incredible as one who works for humanity and not for himself (but we know who Mr. Incredible is *really* working for).

A good type of fund-raiser activity would be a drive to send money for a national cause that the colleges would be familiar with throughout the country or world, possibly a starving country in Asia. As proof of your work, save clippings from the paper or set up a meeting with your board of education, during which you can present the money to the principal or headmaster as photographers take pictures. This can easily reach the city's daily newspaper if you inform them by phone or mail. Remember "the power of the press." Use their power for yourself as you mail your articles to the college in support of your activities. Press coverage, no matter how small, makes the activity seem much more substantial.

Nancy Nurd vs. Suzy Superior

As a young child, Nancy Nurd had been a fanatic of electronic machines and computers. She spent half her life in the computer room at her high school. The other half of her life was spent dreaming of building a computer or planning endless trips to the public library's computer center each weekend. Nancy was a nurd, obviously, and she was too shortsighted to use her knowledge to her advantage. Although she enjoyed her computer talents, she withdrew into herself and refused to share her knowledge as she dreamed of IBM XX4CC Datatrons with Dual Control Terminals for the rest of her life.

Suzy Superior had also spend endless hours with computer programs, but she always had her eye on a college education. In the ninth grade she formed a computer club for students in high school. That summer she took some weekly courses at a local community college on computer programming. Here Suzy received some professional instruction.

By the second semester of tenth grade Suzy was so proficient at the computer that she requested that the board of education allow her to train some younger students in basic computer skills. She gave a weekly one-hour beginner's course for a period of five months. Because Suzy realized that this was an opportunity to enhance her college application, she had a few pictures taken as she instructed the students. She also asked that an article be written in the school newspaper on her minicourse. Her activity naturally improved her relations with the school faculty, who would soon be preparing her college recommendations.

Once Suzy got started, she just couldn't stop. She recognized that with her experience, she could probably add a summer job experience in the computer field to her portfolio. She used the Yellow Pages to call businesses that were computer-oriented and informed them of her experience as a student teacher for computers. Although she landed a minimum-wage paying job in a small computerized technical firm, she was able to show colleges that she was organized and was able to direct her energy toward her strengths (specialization).

In her essays for colleges, she discussed her past experience in the computer field, since she had once played, learned, taught, and even worked in a computer-oriented environment. The admissions office perceived Suzy as a welcome addition to the university's computer-science program.

Although Nancy Nurd and Suzy Superior had equal knowledge of computer programming, Suzy had the foresight to make it work for her college application.

Super Jock vs. Mr. Sportsmanship

The student who is brilliant and is an athlete has a special problem. The character of an intelligent student is often put down if he is also athletic. He is criticized by fellow students as being nothing but a "muscle-headed idiot." No matter how smart he is or where he goes to college, his classmates will remind him that he was sent "care-of the football recruiter." The best he can do is ignore these remarks and accept the best school that takes him. After all, no one's going to believe he got there by merit.

If you *are* a Super Jock but want to appear different and more desirable, you can give yourself that extra dignity seen in Mr. Sportsmanship. A tennis player for eight years, Mr. Sportsmanship played in citywide tournaments each summer. He joined the USTA in order to receive a ranking. His actual ranking is not so important—the importance lies in his ability to now say that he is "ranked by the United States Tennis Association." After tenth grade he helped teach group lessons for youngsters in the city recreation tennis day camp. He entered as many tournaments as possible while still participating as captain of the high school varsity team. By the end of the eleventh grade he had won about four trophies. That summer he began a small tennis-racket restringing service at home. He was not concerned with the profit, which was about forty dollars a week (for only six hours of work). His main concern was to emphasize his great involvement in tennis. With a picture or two in a tournament or standing with his trophies and racket-restringing machine, Mr. Sportsmanship became the admissions office's athlete, entrepreneur, and most of all—tennis pro.

Jane University vs. Dynamique Student

Jane University, a B− student, has always loved playing brass instruments, but she never really excelled in any specific one. Because she was the only girl to play in the brass section of her high school band, she devoted less time to music and more time to her natural talent for writing poetry. Her writing was praised by her English teachers, but she hid her talent and writings in a notebook in her desk drawer.

Dynamique Student, also a B− student, decided to specialize in the trombone because she had never known of a woman trombonist. (This would make her appear that much more unique.) She took private lessons and played in the high school band and orchestra until she was good enough to compete in all-city, all-county, and all-state music competitions. Although she eventually reached all-state, she continued to play in all-city too. (This allows her to list a great number of competitions on her college application.) Dynamique reached for her old poetry and took some nighttime poetry writing lessons during the summer and entered a contest. After winning a small local award in poetry, she was able to write to some small literary magazines and inquire about publishing her material. With a preestablished reputation (the award), Jane was able to convince the magazine to publish her writing. She then sent the published copies to the admissions office. The college literary society and campus journal are always looking for promising people like Dynamique. After all, how would they know that she possessed a unique talent if she had merely told them that she liked to write poetry.

In the meantime Dynamique also played in the amateur orchestras for summer stock musicals and enhanced her reputation in the amateur music field. Whether she played for the college interviewer or sent a tape of a solo, the school realized their own orchestra's need for a fine woman trombonist with a good background.

Joe College vs. Super Collegiate

Joe College was raised at a small public school where he worked hard and received grades of B+ and A–. He was in the spring play twice and painted during his spare time at home. Joe loved to act and paint, but he refused to pursue either activity seriously because he knew he wanted to become an architect.

Super Collegiate was raised at the same school, where he worked hard and received the same grades, but he pursued or at least pretended to pursue (which, according to some, is what basically counts) acting and painting. During the summer after ninth grade Super joined a summer stock program, where he performed in two plays. In the tenth grade he took a course in drama at school, in addition to taking a few theatrical lessons during the year and performing in the school play. The next summer he worked in an art studio and was able to gain some "pointers" for his practice at home in the evenings. At the same time he took art lessons. By the end of the summer he had entered his work in some competitions. During the eleventh grade Super appeared in a leading role in a school play, which his father photographed with a home-movie camera.

The college admissions office is happy to see a student like Super Collegiate, who is able to narrow his interests and channel his energy in order to excel to an above-average level. In circumstances in which a school wants a dramatic or artistic person, Super would easily fit the bill.

Activities like acting will often require that the student use photographic equipment in order to display his talent to the admissions staff. A school is very impressed by a student who goes to great lengths to provide supportive material of activities in such an elaborate manner. The admissions office looks at Joe College as being fairly versatile, whereas Super Collegiate is perceived as a potential benefit to the univeresity drama group or campus art society.

Bill Tenderfoot vs. Senior Scout

Bill Tenderfoot believed in the "free spirit." He had loved the outdoor life ever since he first joined Boy Scouts in the seventh grade, but he never advanced past the first rank. Three years later he now says that although he never advanced and although he worked like a dog while camping and learning first-aid, he did the most important thing—he enjoyed himself. Now Bill is trying to find a job for next fall because he was rejected by all of his colleges. Why? Well, for one reason, he put all his time (including school work time) into the Boy Scouts, thus receiving grades of C–. Another reason was that he had no Scout rank to show his work to the admissions office. Let's see how Bill could have had better luck, even with C– grades.

Senior Scout, a C– student in all of his courses, worked his way up the ranks by doing not just Scout work that was enjoyable but also work that would fulfill merit-badge requirements. Each year he would lead his patrol to win a blue or red ribbon in Scout competitions. He worked on a project with the scoutmaster and ten other young scouts to do lawn work at a neighborhood nursing home and to fill potholes in two playground lots. Senior Scout notified the city newspaper of his community involvement and his plans for a small nature trail. Although he did not partake of the physical labor in all these projects, he did act as a planner and liaison person with publicity. He photo-copied the articles and pictures of the activities and used them to support his college candidacy. His scoutmaster, who was very impressed with Senior Scout's work, was glad to write a favorable recommendation.

Once Senior Scout became Senior Patrol Leader of the troop, he prepared an eight-page report, describing his activities in the Boy Scouts and how the work benefited him, and presented it to his local Boy Scouts Council. The council returned a letter of thanks for his contributions to the organization, thus giving Senior Scout an additional letter to support his applications to colleges. Senior Scout has shown us how you can not only enjoy the outdoors but also use it as a tool in a college admissions plan.

46

Summing Up

Of course you don't have to be a Super Collegiate, a Suzy Superior, or a Mr. Incredible in order to get into a good school. These characters merely exemplify extremes and represent a few possible ways to make yourself look better than the other applicants. Just choose an activity and function somewhere near the "Superior" or "Incredible" level. Whatever you do, don't be a "Nancy Nurd" or a "Joe College" because your lack of talent will drive your college application into a black hole.

What you must truly remember is the importance of choosing an unusual activity and also choosing an activity that you are willing to devote time to excel in and "shine" brightly above others. In order to "shine," you must work hard, enter contests, and narrow your activities in other areas. If you don't find yourself "shining" sufficiently, then you have to make the admissions office think you are—through the use of the neighborhood or school newspaper or snapshots of yourself and your activity. The influence is so much greater when you can provide something more than your word in order to substantiate your comments. Remember that anyone can *say* that he can play a C# harp and swallow fire at the same time, but only a few will actually have pictures and tapes of the memorable event.

When charity donations were mentioned earlier in the chapter, the importance of donating funds at a publicized affair was stressed. If you insist that this takes the benevolence out of your initial act and if you think it makes you appear to be working for yourself, you're wrong. You are not just working for yourself; you are working for your school board or your principal or your coach, and *they*, in turn, "work" for you by writing recommendations. And the recommendation finally "works" toward your acceptance. You'll find out more on how to get the most out of your recommendations in Rule Seven.

Rule Six: Getting Your Application into Shape

Playing this college admissions game can be a lot of fun, but since our main objective is to win, let's not waste any time as we pass this midway mark. This sixth rule is one of the most important because it's where you start your application and essay and just let the "bull" flow freely.

Contrary to popular belief, you can still lead a normal existence while finishing your applications on time. As soon as you learn how to budget your time with a few short cuts, you'll be on your way. You'll find that a comfortable schedule for deadlines will allow you to create a very impressive application.

How to Organize Everything

When you begin receiving the applications, read through each one. As you read, highlight or underline the deadlines for essays, transcripts, SAT scores and interviews. Begin a deadline sheet on a piece of 8½-x-11-inch paper (see Figure 6–1). Since you'll need plenty of space for each school, turn the page sideways and draw horizontal lines to provide space for each school. In the separate columns you can list the address, application deadline, teacher recommendation deadline, transcript deadline, and interview date for each of the colleges you select. Any additional space can be used for supplementary information deadlines or the names of admissions officers. You'll find that this simple information/deadline sheet puts information at your fingertips when you start to panic about your busy schedule. Whether you post it above your desk, on the refrigerator, or in the playroom, this schedule will help you. If you look at the sheet briefly each day, you'll be able to keep up with everything.

After you've listed each of your colleges on the deadline sheet, place all pamphlets and information from each school into a 10-x-15-inch accordion-type folder, labeling each section accordingly. This will allow you to reach for everything on one particular school. Many students just throw every bit of mail in a large drawer or under the bed. The only problem with this is that you might very well be waiting for an application to arrive in the mail when it's actually under stacks of junk on your desk. Keeping everything together takes just a little time. Don't experiment by relying on your memory of deadlines. Avoid secret hiding places for applications and information. The fifteen minutes spent creating this schedule and preparing these folders can save you because most colleges will quickly reject a candidate if material isn't received on time.

Figure 6–1 Deadline Sheet

School	Application deadline	Teacher recommendation	Transcript deadlines	Interview	Misc.
Davis Univ. 6 Redd Rd. Dayton, Oh. 32167	Preliminary due Nov.9/ Regular due Jan.1	2, due 3/15 mr. Smith·History miss Thomas·Math	Guidance counselor sent in already	Jan.13 with Dr.J. Stein, Dir. Admissions	
Bern Coll. P.O.Box 73 Oakville, ma. 02136	Due Dec. 15 (send two copies)	4 teachers + 1 peer (ask Tom)	Handled by school due Dec.20	Call in mid-December to schedule	request course catalog

How to Get Started on the Application

It's best to begin by setting aside about thirty minutes each day after school for your applications. You can add or subtract from your allotted time after the first application, as you see how fast you're able to complete them. For the first few weekends during your application process, allow yourself about four hours for working on applications. Since you've read through each application, you already know the deadlines. Begin working on the college with the earliest deadline for applications.

Before you start writing anything, consider the fact that the colleges frown upon sloppy applications. They don't want to see cross-outs, grease stains, or even creases in their forms. Remember they have to read through tons of essays and forms from all over the country. If yours isn't very appealing, it won't get a good rating. If you don't mind spending the extra money, it's a good idea to photocopy the first two applications. This works well because you can practice on the copies until you're ready to work on the original.

The first couple of pages are general questions concerning your citizenship, date of birth, educational status, parents' names, social security number, etc. Since these general questions are repeated in each college application, make a note of the answers so that you don't waste energy researching them each time. Fill out the first pages of the application lightly in pencil, and check over your answers two or three times to make sure they're correct. Later you can erase the pencil (if you didn't make a copy) and type directly onto the original copy of the application. It is suggested that you type or have someone type for you. If you absolutely must print it, use only black or blue ballpoint pens. To correct your mistakes, keep a bottle of correction fluid on hand.

Once you've reached the point where the college is asking about your major activities, dig back into your list of Extraordinarily Unique Activities from Rule Five and jot them down on another sheet of paper. Unfortunately, this part of the application doesn't really allow you to explain your activities. There is only enough space for the name of the activity. This is where you will have to develop a title for your role in the activity in order to list it properly. If you were a participant in the student government, you will need to develop a "catchy" title for your position. Be reasonable and be honest in your labeling of positions. If your position already has a title, use it on the application.

Another short-answer question will probably deal with your past summer employment. Be as concise as possible; you can use more detail in an extra essay if necessary. You will probably be asked about any traveling you've done or awards you've received. Make sure that you list anything and everything you have accomplished.

Why You Should Never Be Modest

You're probably wondering why you shouldn't be modest. The reason is that if you don't put what you did in the application, the college assumes that you never did it. Colleges don't assume that your family takes a trip to the coast each summer. Although you may think nothing of it, colleges feel that a well-traveled person is a well-rounded person. *Modesty can only hurt you in the end.* Never worry about bragging too much, especially if your grades and scores are low. Even if you won a very small bowling tournament two years ago, mention it in the application. After all, maybe the college is seeking potential bowling stars.

Another important rule is to never leave a question unanswered. If you are asked about foreign travel, think of an answer. Even if it means writing in "domestic travel" or hiking in the hills outside your town, write it down. Blank spaces don't look on an application. Even if your response isn't exactly what the college wants, it's better than no response at all.

Now for the Essays

The essay is where you get the opportunity not only to let the "bull" flow but also to show your mastery of the English language. You ought to know that the essay is your opportunity to go all out to create a good impression. It's a great place to say things you couldn't say face-to-face with an interviewer. Whatever you do with your essay or essays, make them stand out in the crowd of other essays. Spend time to plan them, to edit them, and to reedit them.

Unfortunately, most colleges will dream up outrageous topics for you to write about. This prevents you from beginning the essays before you receive the application. It also prevents you from using the same essay for each school. But you know what? Some schools request two or three essays. One of these two or three is bound to ask general questions about your activities and awards. The general questions usually ask how your activities fit in with your future goals. Essays with general topics like this can be used over and over for almost every college that wants an essay. You might find questions like the following:

1. In two pages, explain how two or three of your main activities have prepared you for the future.
2. If you could relive an experience from your past, what would you choose?
3. Which of your achievements best represents your concern for others?

Each of these questions allows you enough room to discuss your opinions, your goals, and your philosophy. Essays like these are great because you can write pages and pages about yourself. What topic could be easier?

I have always believed that textbooks, lectures and final examinations were only a part of a student's classroom. The real classroom is what I have been exposed to during my life- time. Family trips, music lessons, summer jobs and the high school newspaper are all a part of my classroom. Patience and continued interest have been my teachers in all of these situations.

Two years ago, I became interested in my high school newspaper, The Oak Ridge Journal. While working as a staff writer in the tenth grade, I realized that I had gained a great deal of responsibility. It was expected that all deadlines were to be met. There was no excuse for misquoting sources or vio- lating the rights of others. In this position, I learned to take orders from my editors while also appreciating their ideas.

Within a year and a half, I was appointed Editor-in-Chief of this 42 person newspaper. It was an honor to become the leader of a paper that had just received a "First Place" rating at the National Scholastic Press Association. I found myself in the more important aspects to my appointment. Being a leader is not always position where I had to give orders as well as write articles each issue. I had to protect my editors' First Amendment Rights as well as demand their respect. Being a leader is not always easy because you have to enforce discipline, and yet, keep a good morale among the staff members.

My appreciation for different types of music has made me a better person since I began playing the piano five years ago. While I enjoy listening to the popular songs of today, I can appreciate music of different eras and different cultures. My participation in the all-city orchestra has enabled me to play in competition as well as for enjoyment. If accepted, I would hope to continue playing in the University orchestra. I would also like to give piano lessons to beginning students on campus. I feel that everyone should learn to play as well as enjoy all types of music.

Since I was very young my parents have taken my brother and me on summer vacations. The most eventful trips were thos spent in Martha's Vineyard and Mexico. In Martha's Vineyard, I grew closer to my family as we dug clams in the bay and beach museums. In Mexico, I learned about life outsi feel that it is necessary for all cultures t

Creating the Impressive Essay

Before answering these questions, list the most impressive activities and most interesting jobs or experiences that you want to discuss in depth. Now you should write the essay *around* the topics that you want to bring up. Be able to describe how "Girl Scouts taught you the importance of helping others in need" or "your paper route gave you independence and greater responsibility" or "the track team showed you the importance of team effort." Show the school that every experience was a phase of learning and self-improvement.

Remember that the purpose of the essay is to show that you are unique or better than the average. It is a place to be creative, and it is also a vehicle for conveying an important message to the admissions staff. In the past, some students have tried every method possible to make the college remember their applications. There have been students who used extreme tactics like writing their essay in a foreign language, in calligraphy, or even upside down and backwards. These people just want to draw attention to their candidacy. After all, these preparations and neat ideas *are* helpful because there's a possibility that you will come up against another student with the same grades and scores as you have. The only thing that can distinguish you from the other applicant is your application. If yours doesn't stand out, the admissions officers may very well select the other person. Although your application doesn't have to be outlandish, don't take the risk of sending in a dull application that displays no character. Use some of the ideas outlined in Rule Five to make your essay Extraordinarily Unique.

Finishing Touches for the Essay

If you find your essay isn't long enough, you better add to it by simply recalling more of your experiences. When you are writing, don't worry about proper grammar or correct spelling. As a matter of fact, it's better not to worry about exceeding the desired length at first. You can always go back and edit later. When you're done, you can check through everything with a dictionary and a thesaurus. For those of you who are weak in grammar, it's all right to bring the essay to your English teacher for specific problems. This is acceptable as long as the teacher doesn't write the essay for you. When you're absolutely satisfied with your "work of art," type it neatly on the form or on your own high-quality, erasable typing paper. You may want to photocopy one or two of your essays for two reasons:

1. You may have to repeat some of the same profound sentences or paragraphs in another essay, and

2. You may never be able to make yourself look so good on paper again. When written in a foreign language, or in calligraphy, these essays make nice conversation pieces.

Once you've written a school's essays, make sure that they are neither too long nor too short. Make sure you "cram" in all the little extras that you'd like to mention. If there's any doubt that you should mention something, then mention it. When you're satisfied with content and length, read it to yourself and then aloud. If you don't have someone to read it to you, then tape-record it and play it back. This will allow you to add important information and eliminate unnecessary words. Most college admissions staff members read these essays aloud to one another. So why not use their method and beat them at their own game!

Do's and Don'ts of the Essay

Although many of the mistakes created in the essay are made because you are rushing to meet deadlines, other problems can still arise even when you aren't rushing. Read through your essay and see if you only gabbed on about yourself. You'll be able to tell very easily. If every sentence begins with "I did this" or "I believe . . ." or "I feel . . .," bring in other ideas and other people besides yourself. Another thing to consider is the importance of showing the college what *you* can do for *them*. How you can add to or help the student body is something that they look for in each student's application. Don't devote the entire essay to explaining how their college can help you. Even if you are primarily interested in improving *your* computer skills at a college, use the essay to explain your desire to tutor others with basic computer skills. Show that the school can benefit from your talents too.

The essay is where you can acknowledge your weaknesses. Since the college will eventually see your low grades, you can get a jump on them and give your excuses now. Students justify low grades by explaining that they had to work after school to support themselves or that they had spread themselves too thin by joining too many activities and charity groups. A college admires the student who looks at himself objectively and realizes his own mistakes. This shows them that you have the possibility of "straightening out" when you finally attend college. Frequently, high school students get overinvolved with boy-girl relationships and lose sight of their academic goals. If this is the case, explain it in your essay. You can only gain points when you explain your mistakes. If you say nothing about your low grades, the colleges will only assume that you aren't capable of improving.

Play It Safe with the Mail

When mailing your application to the college, make sure that you have the proper postage. If you can afford the extra cost, it's better to mail it with a certified delivery. This way you are sent an acceptance note, which assures you that the application was received by the correct person. Why waste months waiting for an acceptance letter when you're not even sure that all of your colleges received your applications and essays? Don't take any chances.

Supplementary Material

After your application is sent in, you might win new awards or join new organizations. It's good to drop a typed letter to each of the colleges and let them know what you're doing before they make their final decisions. This also serves as a reminder to them that you still desperately want to attend their college. Your intention is to keep your name in the forefront of the applicants. People have been known to send in photographs, recipes, homemade gourmet cakes, tape recordings of a piano lesson, computer printouts, and everything else under the sun to grab the college's attention. If you don't mind putting out the extra postage, send them something that you wrote, discovered, or created.

Record Keeping

When you have made sure that your guidance counselor has sent your high school grades to your colleges and when you have completed all of the applications and essays, go back to your schedule and write down the day that the material was mailed. This serves as a record if the mail gets lost on its way to the college. Any other supplementary material should also be checked off and listed on your schedule.

It's still not time to sit back and rest because we have to enlist the help of others. In Rule Seven you'll learn that friends, teachers, and employers will help you get into the college of your choice.

Rule Seven: Touching Bases with Recommendations and Contacts

You've all heard the saying "It's not what you know, it's who you know." This phrase is also important when you're applying to college and need help to get in. Although this sounds very cynical, it's really not. People use connections and contacts in everyday life. So how can "dropping" someone's name and using his clout be wrong? Unfortunately, the use of contacts and name dropping can get people into trouble when done improperly. In this rule you'll learn how to get recommendations from teachers and other people who count. With the aid of these few pages, you will learn not only *how* to use contacts for job seeking and everyday situations but also *whom* to contact for the greatest letters of recommendation.

Once you've received the college applications, check to see how many recommendations each college wants. Most colleges want to see what other people think about you—as a student, a person, an employee, and even as a best friend. Although many colleges specifically ask for a letter of recommendation from a teacher, many other colleges want your employer or your orchestra or dance instructor to evaluate your character, ability, and attitude. There are several schools that request a friend your own age to write about his perception of you.

Seven Requirements for Finding Great Letter Writers

Since all this sounds so simple, you probably think that you can ask anyone for a recommendation. Unfortunately, it's not easy at all because no matter whom you ask, there are several considerations:

1. Does the person (employer, teacher, etc.) respect me as an employee, student, etc.?
2. Does the person like my personality?
3. Does the person appear sufficiently enthusiastic to write a positive recommendation?
4. Does the person remember my being in his class or working in his business?
5. Can this person express himself clearly with concise language?
6. Does this person have the time to carefully write a page-long letter?
7. Will this person forget to write the letter, forget to mail the letter, or forget who I am?

You should ask yourself these seven questions about each person you approach. The best way to strike out is to ignore these questions. If you can't answer "yes" to each of them, it's time to look for another reference. Let's look into each of these questions and see how and why we must use them. Since it's important to make the best possible impression on each college, a bad recommendation will only elicit a rejection letter.

Requirement One

Does the person (employer, teacher, etc.) respect me as an employee, student, etc.?

Let's review this first question. You might wonder how one knows if his employer or teacher respects him. There are many ways to tell. If your teacher and employer takes the time to carefully correct your work and gives you interesting and challenging work, then he or she respects your abilities. If the person asks your opinion about issues or problems or applauds you when you've worked hard on an additional project, you can tell that you have earned his respect. These are the people who will emphasize, in a college letter, your intelligence, honesty, and academic promise.

Requirement Two

Does this person like my personality?

Now that you've answered the first question, how do you answer the second? The way to tell if a teacher or employer likes your personality is through his or her remarks. A person who likes you will enjoy your humor and be sympathetic to your problems. This teacher or employer is also one who shares his emotions and concerns with you. This is the teacher or employer who can tell the college about the kindness and friendliness that you display toward others.

Requirement Three

Does this person appear sufficiently enthusiastic to write a positive recommendation?

The third question is rather easy to answer since it depends upon the initial reaction by the person that you ask to recommend your candidacy. If he displays the least bit of doubt about writing the letter, it might be better to start looking elsewhere. Avoid people who make remarks like, "Well, Miriam, I'll write it if you've got absolutely no one else" or "Are you sure I'm the best one to recommend you?" or "To tell you the truth, Jeremy, I really hate writing these things, but I guess I better." The ideal person will answer you with "Oh Betty, I'm flattered that you want me to write for you. I'll do it as soon as you need it" or "Of course I will, Greg; I love to write for my best students." Once you've found this reaction, you're on your way.

Requirement Four

Does the person remember me being in his class or working in his business?

Frequently, teachers and employers pay no attention to those around them and can't even name their students and employees. This is why we ask ourselves the fourth question. It is recommended that you approach only those people who have worked with you within the past two years. If you dig back any further than two years, you might find that the teacher has forgotten your classroom contributions. The employer who writes a good recommendation is one who recalls your initiative and dependability on the job. Don't bother with the teacher or employer who never really knew *you* or *your* work.

Requirement Five

Can this person express himself clearly with concise language?

You can usually be sure of finding an articulate faculty member to write a grammatically correct letter. The fifth question primarily warns us against the person who *cannot* write a positive letter in perfect English. Since colleges evaluate their applicants, they also evaluate the applicants' letter-writers. Although the person may have good intentions, he may not have the ability to express all of your positive characteristics and achievements.

Requirement Six

Does this person have the time to carefully write a page-long letter?

The sixth question is very essential because many teachers and employers are asked to write many other letters of recommendation. A person will often come right out and tell you he has no time to write a letter. Sometimes he'll hint to you by saying, "Well, Leslie, I'll try to whip through it during my coffee break or on the train ride home." Some teachers might even say, "Not you too? I'll do it. But, Richard, I might as well write the same letter for both you and Charlie, if you don't mind." Take this as a hint that the teacher is just too rushed to write a good recommendation. Don't waste your time insisting that the person "squeeze" it into his schedule.

Requirement Seven

Will this person forget to write the letter, forget to mail the letter, or forget who I am?

The last of the seven questions is one of the easiest to answer. Almost anyone can identify the absentminded teacher who almost forgets his head when going to class. If you have the slightest suspicion that your teacher or boss forgets deadlines or loses papers, don't give him the opportunity to forget your recommendation. You'll only be crucifying yourself if you entrust your college candidacy to such a careless person. Many a student is rejected because the admissions office never receives the required letters of recommendation. Don't give yourself any of these problems. Take precautions by finding someone who can answer a "yes" to all seven of these questions.

How Many Recommendations and Whom Can You Ask?

Although most colleges request two letters of recommendation, students continue to ask how many letters are *really* necessary. It is often said that you can never have too many letters, but you *can* have the *wrong type* of letters. Assuming that each of your letter-writers has cleared the seven questions, you can ask almost anyone you know. To give you an idea, here's a list of people to consider:

actors	music instructors	team coaches
athletes	dance instructors	den mothers/scoutmasters
writers	college alumni	rabbis or ministers
doctors	guidance counselors	college professors
teachers	club advisers	editors
principals	camp directors	politicians
employers	distant relatives	wealthy benefactors

Out of this long list, you should certainly find a few people to write a letter on your behalf. Some of you are probably asking how each of these people could really help your candidacy. You may not realize it, but even your school custodian could write you a winning recommendation. After all, it's not entirely who they are, it's also how well they know and like you.

Case Studies

Although Anita was applying to Oberlin College for the arts and sciences program, she knew that the school had a great drama department. Since her father had grown up with a B-rated actor who played in an off-Broadway show, she asked for the actor's assistance. She asked him to evaluate her as she performed a fifteen-minute Shakespearean soliloquy. Although she had never really performed previously, Anita did well enough to obtain a brief letter of recommendation from the actor. She asked him to write something that emphasized her (almost) natural talent for Shakespeare. Even though this seems like an outrageous strategy, it worked for Anita's candidacy.

Sam was desperate for a strong letter of recommendation because his grades and scores were below the mean of his target school—the University of Arizona. The last resort was his trumpet teacher. Sam had been playing for only three years, but he requested a recommendation that commented on his persistence and determination. Sam knew that this would be a good reflection on him because it signified that he would also be persistent and determined in his studies once Arizona accepted him. Colleges look for the persevering student who never reaches great heights but keeps on plugging. Although Sam was no all-city finalist, he had potential and he put everything into his work. If you can show a college this characteristic, the admissions officers are usually very willing to believe in your determination.

Lia was ready to kill when she found out that her principal forgot to send in her Skidmore College letter of recommendation. She now had less than two weeks to find someone to write for her. The only thing Lia could think of was to call up Skidmore and ask for the school's alumni association in her area. While looking through the list, she found that her old pediatrician had attended the school. Lia immediately called her doctor and renewed old ties by explaining how much she wanted to be a part of Skidmore. Her doctor was glad to write the letter and was pleased that Lia liked Skidmore College. Alumni are often very powerful because they are the main financial supports of their colleges. You get extra points for the rich alumni who give large sums of money each year—they wield lots of clout in the admissions office!

Carl was very close to his minister since he attended church regularly and sang in the choir. He was looking forward to studying religion and sociology at Tulane University in Louisiana. He had been a church volunteer and had raised money at seven of the annual fund raisers. Carl's commitment to help others and his desire to learn more about religion in today's society pleased his minister. Carl decided that it was his minister who knew him best, and therefore he asked him to write a letter about Carl's contributions to the church and to his surroundings.

Earlene had been friends with Leora since they had been in junior high school. When it came time for Leora to apply to Wesleyan College, she was asked to provide a peer recommendation. Earlene was the person to write it because she admired her friend and recognized Leora's good and bad qualities. Because of their true friendship, Leora received a well-written recommendation from someone who knew her well.

You can see how a recommendation can be written by many different types of people. What matters is the topics that they discuss and the way they present you as a person. If you can get quality recommendations like the above, you might as well collect as many as three or four for each school.

How to Ask a Person to Write a Recommendation

Now that you know whom to ask, let's learn *how* to ask. The old saying "The early bird catches the worm" is most applicable when considering how soon you should approach someone for a recommendation. It's really never too early to ask for a letter as long as you ask politely. The proper time is when the person is not pressed by deadlines. But ask him when others are not present. Without presenting him with any forms or resumes, begin by talking about your interest in a particular college. Then ask him politely if he would have the time to write a letter on your behalf. If necessary, catch the person during the lunch break. This is a time when people are most relaxed and most likely to agree to your request. Let's take a look at Damon's method for asking his history teacher.

DAMON: *Mr. Fearon, may I ask you something about the history department?*

MR. FEARON: *Why certainly, Damon. What would you like to know?*

DAMON:	*Well, I'm really interested in history and I'll probably major in it at college. I'm a little confused about the principal periods in European history. Most schools that I've looked at offer European history before the Civil War period. If I'm thinking about becoming a history professor, which period is more valuable as a background?*
MR. FEARON:	*Damon, I'm really glad to see you're that interested in history, and I'm also flattered that you're asking for my opinion. For the present day, the post-Civil War period is most important because the trends in Europe today seem only to repeat those of the late 1800s.*
DAMON:	*So, in that case, the University of Georgia would be my best choice. By any chance, would you mind writing a brief recommendation for me, since you know of my interest in history?*
MR. FEARON:	*Of course I don't mind. Especially since you've done all of this research on your future. History is a great topic to study.*

Two days later, Damon brought his recommendation form and a self-addressed, stamped envelope to his teacher. He made the procedure as simple as possible for his teacher. He even penciled the deadline date on the back of the envelope.

Making It Easy for the Letter-Writer

It's a good idea to provide your letter-writer with a typewritten summary of your activities, awards, interests, and goals. In that way the person can add these personal touches to a letter that already evaluates your character and your abilities as a student. Don't be presumptuous by handing all of this material to the person as soon as he agrees to recommend you. It's best to wait a day or two so that he doesn't think you're rushing him. Express your appreciation of his agreement to recommend you.

There are many colleges that ask you to waive your rights to see the recommendation. You should abide by this rule. It shows the letter-writer that you trust and and respect his opinion. For those colleges that don't provide you with a special form, give the teacher two or three sheets of twenty-five-pound erasable, high-quality paper. Once the reference writer sees that you've taken a lot of trouble, he will take a lot of trouble to write a good letter.

A Word on Contacts

Some of us are lucky enough to have parents and relatives who know people on the admissions staffs or have contacts at the colleges. Don't be afraid of using these connections. Ask your parents to call them and politely inform them of your application to that particular college. Don't ask for any special favors. Just have Mom or Dad ask them something like "How should my daughter apply for an interview?" or "Who handles the information sessions?" Once they've started the conversation like this, have them slowly lead the contact into offering any help he can give.

Important Do's and Don'ts

No matter whom you ask to write for you, there are certain things you must know. You must follow up by reminding the people of the deadline. It's easy to do this by calling them up and asking them if they have the address of the college. This is a polite way to find out if they have mailed it. Another technique is to drop them a thank-you note a week before the deadline. Not only will this remind those who have forgotten, but it will also serve as a genuine thank you for those who have remembered. It's *not* wise to pay for or to buy a gift for those letter-writers (before or after) because they will look upon your gift as a bribe or a kickback. These people are usually satisfied with the thought that you respected their ability to evaluate your character. They are genuinely flattered.

Now that you've followed through with this seventh rule, you can enter the eighth phase of the application process. Rule Eight will show you some practice methods for the college interview and some interview strategies that never fail.

Rule Eight: How to Score with the On-Campus Interview

An on-campus interview is often the clincher for an outgoing, personable student who can effectively impress the cynical admissions officer. Schools that don't require interviews can be a blessing to the soft-spoken, shy student who has difficulty communicating. If this description fits your personality, be realistic and don't ask for an interview if it's not required.

Start in April or early May of your junior year to call schools for interviews. This is enough time to arrange an interview at the most popular schools. If the school runs out of vacant appointments, the admissions officers might inform you of their group sessions. If this option is offered, you'll be wasting your time unless you're merely in need of information about the school. Remember, the purpose of an interview is to *sell* yourself, to make yourself look like God's gift to that particular college. Needless to say, you want to flatter the school when necessary and develop a "familiar relationship" with the officer so that he remembers you when your application is discussed during the selection process.

Preparing Your Artillery

Before you get to the interview, you will need to prepare your *artillery*. This means the topics you plan to casually bring up in conversation. Casual topics actually consist of previously well-researched information on the school (deeper information than what appears in their public relations pamphlets): its history, curriculum, student activities, famous professors, noted graduates, social meeting places, and even geographical environment. You should be able to speak about these topics, but don't sound too knowledgeable because interviewers can detect a snow job when a student can list twenty famous alumni and name the year that the admissions office was established. Prior to the interview, you might also want to thumb through the schools' current sports records in the newspaper and note the teams' weaknesses. If you have any athletic abilities in their weak areas, during your interview stress your talent in that sport or build on your talent, and, if need be, create the talent! Tell the interviewer that you have always enjoyed playing ——, but your high school had such a small program that it was just not feasible to play —— because of the lack of any other talent. Let's face it, many large schools, like the University of Michigan and Cornell, will do most anything for a great ball player with a B or B– average.

When you go to the interview, bring a portfolio with examples of your work or awards that you have received. This portfolio should be a regular album with pictures of you performing a solo in an all-county orchestra, interviewing the mayor for your high school newspaper, or even standing in a modest pose in front of your bowling trophies. Any published articles that you have written should also be included.

Your Uniform

Another important aspect of the interview process is your physical appearance. Let's assume that you have good grooming habits. But let's also assume (hope) that you haven't just arrived from Bergdorf Goodman's hair salon or the Chanel parfumerie in Paris. As far as clothing is concerned, shoes rather than tennis sneakers are a necessity. They show a respect for the officer and for yourself. One should not wear jeans under any circumstances, even those with the new designer labels; to the older members of the admissions staffs, jeans are still jeans. Men should stick to the fairly conservative sport jacket and plain button-down shirts. A tie too often looks as if Dad dressed you. Women should wear skirts and casual blouses for simplicity. Both males and females should wear clothing that is plain

Of course you want to show that you are individual, at ease with yourself, and able to stand apart from the crowd, but if you choose worn jeans, hair untempered by brush or razor, home-crafted jewelry that is better placed on exhibit, and tennis shoes whose only distinction is their stripe, an admissions officer may be hard placed to discern the individuality you proclaim.

Style is how you represent yourself: if you show up for your interview aping the straight, buttoned-up look of a corporate executive or emblazoned with your old school crest, the interviewer will know at a glance that you represent someone other than yourself.

In order to look good, you don't have to emulate the good taste that has become codified in the "preppy" look. Clothes that reflect you but are comfortable, well-chosen, and suitable for a friendly but formal discussion of who you
are and how you plan to define your life are your best support.

so that it doesn't distract the interviewer. The simplicity prevents the interviewer from drawing too many conclusions about your personal tastes.

Parents and the Interview

Make sure that your parents do not join you in the interview—even if the officer asks them. Just ask both of them to give a kind refusal. Why? Because (not to offend your "pushy" or concerned parents) they'll blow it for you with their "innocent" comments, interruptions, and even facial expressions. How do you expect to get away with "half-truths" if they are there to correct your errors? Sara, a high school student, was a victim of her father's mouth during her interview at Smith College. As Sara tried to comment on her volunteer experience in social activities, her father interrupted:

INTERVIEWER: *As you must know, Sara, we at Smith have always looked for young ladies who not only have done for themselves but also have given to others, voluntarily.*

SARA: *Why yes, I have always believed in the same ideals, and that's why for the past four summers I've given two months of my time to the Sacred Hollow Hill Day Care Center where I have—*

DADDY: *Sara, honey, you forget that was only three years. Last summer [proudly to the interviewer] I gave Sara a high-paying job in the office where she oversaw the billing and repossessing of furniture from tenants in my eight subsidized housing projects. Daddy's little girl did a great job, more than she could ever do for any day care center. She worked on so—*

SARA: *Oh, Daddy! Mrs. Jones doesn't want to hear about your housing projects.*

DADDY: *Of course, dear, I just wanted her to know that you have worked in responsible positions.*

As we can easily see, Sara has been caught in a small "half-truth." Her career at Smith was ruined before she got out of the interview. This is one example of a parent who really blew it! If you have one of these "you-are-going-to-get-into-college-if-it-kills-me" parents, then it is best to first collaborate on how much of the truth you later plan to expose. After all, it takes just a little slip of the tongue for the interviewer to see that he's got a loser.

Analyzing the Interviewer

To prepare yourself as a good subject for an interview, you must learn to be perceptive. You really must be able to tell the officer what he wants to hear while also appealing to his personality. You can identify his personality through his physical appearance, office arrangement, word usage, etc. Your main goal is to make him feel comfortable so that you can gain a favorable recommendation. If he is sloppily dressed, poorly groomed, and works in an office that looks like a national disaster, assume that he is a slob. So treat him like one. Slobs are annoyed by meticulously neat and well-groomed people. With this in mind, act relaxed (don't mind slouching). Compliment him on his office, remarking on how personal it is (and use the word *intimate* if you are a female). Sloppy people have very poor social manners, so show no surprise if he wipes his nose on his sleeve—just pretend not to notice. Most important, don't be overly polite because your tact will probably clash with his rudeness. He might envy polite people. Just relax and play the game.

Facing the Interviewer

Upon meeting the admissions officer, introduce yourself while standing a good distance (about twelve feet) away from your parents. This presents an air of independence, a trait that is very important to interviewers. After entering the interviewer's office, wait until he seats you; then you can comment briefly on the train ride or the heat outside. Superfluous conversation is necessary in order to "break the ice." After your remark, let the interviewer ask the important questions. The first pertinent statement will probably be "Well, tell me about yourself." The corresponding response shouldn't be given immediately like a timed bomb; you should give a light laugh and say something like, "Well, where should I start?" Don't let the interviewer answer this question; it is merely rhetorical. Immediately say, "I'm seventeen years old this May and have a twelve-year-old sister. My father is a pharmacist and my mother is a grade school teacher. I attend Oceanside School for the Gifted Child in Peakinville, Wisconsin, where I play the harp in. . . . " Remember not to ask about the interviewer's background.

Also, don't discuss the same subject too long unless the interviewer shows an interest. If he shows a great interest in something specific, then immediately skip to some of your less impressive attributes. This is important because he'll be so curious and engrossed by the previously mentioned topic that he'll ignore those less important topics that follow. Although these topics are not of interest to the interviewer, they do serve a great purpose. They appear to add to the impressive image that you have previously presented—a very active student. Once you've satisfied his curiosity about the topic that most interested him, stop talking. Do this because he'll soon pick up on your plans to impress him with one or two quality activities and a bulk of others in between.

It is important not to appear nervous but to display an air of confidence before the interviewer. Always pretend that each interview is your first so that the interviewer will credit you with your social ease and, at the same time, excuse any of your foolish remarks because he believes you've had no interview experience. Sit back and try to be or pretend to be comfortable. But don't become so relaxed that you say the wrong thing.

Modifying the Conversation for Each School

It's helpful to talk to some students at the school to find out what's happening on the campus. This will convince the interviewer that you are so "into" the campus action that you have already subscribed to their newspaper. Find out from these students some of the major advantages of that school and casually bring these assets up at the interview while favorably comparing them to the drawbacks in other schools of the same caliber. In other words, without telling him, lead the officer to believe that his school is your first choice and nothing less.

Steven, an applicant to several top schools, followed this advice and formulated a different but believable conversation for each school's interview. He stressed only the benefits of each school, whether he saw them as benefits or not.

At Brown University he told Admissions Officer One:

STEVEN: *I want to attend a school in the East that is rather liberal in its outlook toward education, where responsible students are treated as such and are allowed to fulfill the course curriculum that they set for themselves. I must admit that I am an independent student and need the freedom that Brown's open-requirement system allows. As my first choice, Brown . . .*

At Harvard University, he told Admissions Officer Two:

STEVEN: *I need and want the discipline of a core or closed-requirement system because I know that I wouldn't handle freedom properly when it comes to course selections. Although I enjoy many subjects, I like math so much that I would never allow time to take a language. Harvard would add discipline and also make me a well-rounded person. Being my first choice . . .*

At Antioch College he told Admissions Officer Three:

STEVEN: *My main concern in the selection of a school is that it have a small student body and be in a small town. I want to attend a school that will allow me to improve my writing skills on a personal basis as only Antioch can offer. I have to be in a small town away from distractions. This makes Antioch my first choice, and not only does it have. . . .*

At University of California at Los Angeles he told Admissions Officer Four:

STEVEN: *I am in definite need of the cultural boom and excitement of busy Los Angeles so that I can meet interesting students and learn not only from the class but also from the city and its people. UCLA has always been my first choice. . . .*

At Duke University, Steven's "sure" school, Admissions Officer Five knew that Steven was applying to Harvard so he suspected that Duke wasn't Steven's first choice. Steven realized this, so he covered himself:

STEVEN: *I am so glad my parents didn't insist on coming to this interview because although they're willing to let me attend any school I want, they are prejudiced against southern schools. They foolishly think that the good schools are only in the Northeast. They want me to go to Duke if I want to, but they insist that I won't get in because I am not from the South. So they insisted that I apply to good northeastern schools like Harvard, which I could never attend [Steven kept a straight face]. I want to get away from the back-stabbing competition that is so prevalent in the northeastern schools. Duke shows that it trusts the integrity of the students by its use of the honor code. And since I have relatives in Durham, it is the perfect choice. . . .*

Violà, the officer is satisfied that Steven really likes Duke. Steven was able to bring out the good points of each school and indicate why he preferred certain aspects. Once a student can do this, he'll even use this technique in job interviews.

Tricks to Keep the Conversation Going

If you're not the modest type and find yourself talking constantly about your attributes, at least keep close eye contact with the officer to assure him that you are interested in his responses. You could accidentally give him the impression that you give the same spiel to all the schools—eye contact can prevent this. For those of you who find it difficult to look at the interviewer's eyes, especially when bending the truth, stare at his or her nose. This is a very effective way of projecting an honest and serious attitude. And not only is it fun for you but it looks sincere to the interviewer. Sounds crazy, but remember, the nose is so close to the eyes that this method is foolproof.

Once you find yourself running out of topics for conversation, try to remember a subject that you have read about in the school's public relations material. Ask a question about it, but make sure you know the main points and ask the question in such a way that you appear to have only a vague idea of what you're asking about. If, for instance, you're being interviewed for Princeton and you lose your train of thought, but are only able to recall their method of class organization, you could say something like: "I am a little confused about something you might clarify for me. I was reading about a type of class started by Woodrow Wilson at Princeton that is called a conceptorial [actually perceptorial]. Could you please explain its use?" By using the incorrect word (although you really know the correct word) the interviewer realizes that you are sincere in your ignorance, but he is also led to believe that you have at least a vague knowledge of what you're talking about because you mentioned Princeton's favorite namesake, Woodrow Wilson.

The purpose of asking about something you actually know the answer to is to keep the interviewer talking and to stall for time. This technique will give you the opportunity to conjure up another interesting and relevant topic to discuss: a method most effective for long-winded interviewers who enjoy answering ridiculous questions.

If you become bored during the interview, never look at your watch. As a matter of fact, do everything possible to disguise your weariness, or the interviewer will feel insulted and display his hostility in his recommendation. If he's a big talker, act interested by nodding your head and smiling just before you expect him to smile. Laugh at his jokes, especially when he laughs. It seems hypocritical, but remember that he has an ego too, and, more important, he calls the shots!

Post-Interview Strategies

When the interview has ended, make sure that you've satisfied the officer's curiosity about your education and outside activities. Ask him if he could mail you information on the newspaper's freshman program or any other upcoming programs so that your name is reinforced in his memory even after the interview is over. Thank him at the end of the interview and send along a thank-you note as soon as possible. You might want to remind him who you are by adding a friendly but descriptive postscript like, "P.S. I was finally able to talk with the coach of the fencing team and sign up for the news journal program." This is useful because the officers have so many interviews with applicants that they can easily forget names between the time of the interview and the selection process.

Now that you've survived the interview, you can breathe easier and prepare for the "judgment day" with Rule Nine.

Ten Questions Interviewers Ask

During the college interview process, you'll come across interviewers that will ask you hundreds of questions. Many of them are basic questions, but they are used to steer a conversation in a certain direction. In other words, most of the typical "yes" or "no" questions will require more than a simple "yes" or "no." You should expect to explain what you say. Here are some popular questions to prepare you.
  1. Why do you want to attend college?
  2. What can *you* do for XXXX College once you're accepted?
  3. What do you think you'll be doing in about 10 years from now?
  4. What do you think was your most valuable experience?
  5. What type of relationship do you have with your family?
  6. If you could be granted three wishes, what would you ask for?
  7. How do you spend your free time?
  8. What are the most important things that high school has taught you?
  9. Is XXXX College your first choice? Why or Why not?
  10. What is your opinion about [some issue of current interest]?

Rule Nine: After Sliding In or Striking Out

Now that you've done everything you can to get in, you can wait until decision time in April (or December, if you applied for early decision). Some of you, though, might wonder if there's anything you can still do.

As Rule Six, Getting Your Application into Shape, mentioned, it's important that your name be kept in the admissions officers' memories. Without becoming obnoxious, you can continue to send supplementary material or information as frequently as every two weeks (provided that the information is worth sending). By no means should you feel obligated to send extra material, especially if the final decision is to be rendered within three weeks. But remember that the impression you make on the admissions committee is most effective if your name is constantly raised before and during the final selection process.

Also, during this waiting period, you can solicit additional recommendations. Who knows? You may wind up finding a rich alumnus from your favorite college to write a recommendation during those last few weeks.

Waiting for That Letter

You may find yourself waiting, waiting, waiting, and waiting some more before the letters are sent by the colleges. Fortunately there are many colleges that make decisions before the normal April reporting date. You might find acceptances or rejections as early as March or December if you applied for an early decision. Even if you don't receive any notifications from colleges before April, don't panic. Too many students allow fellow classmates to provoke unnecessary tension and anxiety during these last weeks. Many situations can arise that make it difficult to deal with this waiting period. Just don't allow yourself to fall into the trap that caught Carrie.

Carrie had been waiting patiently to hear from Pomona College in California. As early April rolled around, her friends and classmates began receiving their acceptances. Some of her friends asked her if she was nervous about getting into schools "especially since everyone else has been accepted someplace." This was enough to send Carrie into nervous convulsions. After that, she would race home every day to get the mail after school. Daily, Carrie would wrestle the mailman's bag away from him to reassure herself that he wasn't playing tricks on her. Carrie became so upset that she often drove to the village post office to plead with postal workers to allow her to search for her acceptance or rejection letter. Well, you might wonder where Carrie is now. She's probably still jimmying locks off mailboxes on dark street corners. Don't allow yourself to be tormented by anxious classmates or friends. If you're really *that* desperate to see your letter, call the admissions office and ask if all the letters have been mailed. Save yourself the pain of searching for a letter that hasn't even been sent.

Using Spare Time to Locate Financial Aid

As tuition costs soar, so does our need to find new resources for scholarships and financial aid. Now that you're waiting for the colleges to respond, you can spend your time searching for the many grants and scholarships that help pay for those future bills.

Since college admission doesn't stop with being accepted by a college, you have to know the various ways of getting the money to pay for those four years. If you're very rich, don't worry. If you're not rich, don't worry either. There is plenty of money out there, but it's up to you to find it. This book will identify the places to look and the ways to apply for aid.

Often you'll hear a story about the John Doe who was accepted by several top schools but couldn't afford to go, so he never got a college education. Unfortunately this happens, but it won't happen to you if you follow the information provided for you here.

The Financial-Aid Form

If you feel that you will be in need of financial assistance, apply for it. Some people avoid financial aid because they're too proud to accept. The answer for them is that their own tax dollars make the money available, so why not use it if they're eligible? After all, each application is kept confidential. The best excuse people use for avoiding financial aid is that they are too confused by the forms for application. It's true that they're confusing, but that's only to discourage you from applying. So why let the financial aid administration succeed at their tactics. There is really only one confusing form: the Financial-Aid Form (FAF). You can pick this form up from your high school guidance counselor after December 1 of each year. This aid is awarded on the basis of need. At first glance, the form looks like a conglomeration of questions and blank spaces. When you take a closer look, you'll notice that everything is numbered in a logical order. If you're still confused, ask your guidance counselor for help or call the toll-free number on the form and nag the devil out of those people at the other end until they answer your questions. The form will be due on the date specified on your college applications.

The BEOG and SEOG

Next on the list of financial-aid investigation is the federal government's Basic Educational Opportunity Grant Program (BEOG). Since this is a grant, you do not have to repay it. You have the opportunity to receive a fixed amount of money for each year of college, depending on your family's income. Like the BEOG, the Supplemental Educational Opportunity Grants (SEOG) is not repaid to the government. The SEOG can award additional funds for each year of schooling. Other easy-to-apply-for grants can be discovered at the college financial-aid office or at your school's guidance office.

Loans for College

In addition to grants, there are two very popular loan programs: the National Direct Student Loans (NDSL) and the Guaranteed Student

Loan Program (GSLP). Since these are loans, they must be paid back. The NDSL is a no-interest loan program for the time when you are in college. Once you've graduated, the interest rate is set at a low percentage. The GSLP also is a no-interest loan program for the school period. Nine months after graduation, you are to begin repaying the loan at a seven percent interest rate. The great thing about the GSLP is that you can borrow several thousand dollars.

For those of you who want that extra bit of help, there is the College Work Study Program, which creates college jobs on campus for students. These jobs are set aside for students who apply and qualify for the program.

Aid from Your State

While you're checking on federal programs for financial aid, look into what your state has to offer. Each year, at least eight hundred million dollars are spent by the states to assist students. Although all of this information is in your high school counselor's office, you'll probably never find out unless you pin your counselor to the wall. You can often get money from your state for attending a college there.

Scholarship Search Services

In the past few years organizations have been formed to search for scholarships for students who pay a fee for this service. (See Appendix for Search Services). The computerized information is supplied once you have provided the group with information about your grades, scores, family, ethnic group, religion, home state, etc. Once the group has searched for a designated number of scholarships for which you would be eligible, it's up to you to write or to call the various scholarship sponsors.

There are other special grants, scholarships, loans, and services offered for the student. They are listed in the Appendix at the end of this book and it's up to you to apply for them. Although it will take some letter writing, it will be worth the extra thousands you'll eventually receive. With this simplified description of what's available you can look for aid at an even pace during and after the selection process.

Finding Out Where You Stand

It is hoped that the beginning of the financial-aid search has taken your mind away from the college letters. As the letters begin to come in, you can find yourself in many different situations for many different reasons. The most important thing to remember is not to lose your head over rejections. It's not a personal insult to your character if your grades or scores kept you from being accepted by your favorite college. Of course you'll say that "everyone else got accepted by their favorite college." Don't believe your classmates. Don't believe a word they say. Everyone wants to pretend that he got in everywhere he applied. You can tell your classmates whatever you please because they're using the same strategy.

One of the most common situations is the one in which everyone swears he would never apply to a prestigious college. Of your ten friends who swore they never looked twice at Harvard, there's no doubt that eight of them applied and were all flatly rejected. Since people have a tendency to make others think they never lose, you must learn to take their remarks with a grain of salt.

A Situation—Accepted by Every School

If you're lucky enough to have been accepted by all the schools you applied to, you should have nothing to complain about. On the other hand, there are two things that might bother you: (1) the thought that since you got in everywhere, you should have applied to more selective and prestigious colleges or (2) the problem of choosing among acceptances. To the second "problem," most of us would say, "I should be so lucky." But what happens to the student who is accepted everywhere but never really had a first or second choice? Since most colleges allow you only a few weeks to decide on your final choice, you have to work quickly and act decisively.

A Case Study—Accepted Everywhere

Kim had recently received letters of acceptance from Syracuse, Drake, Southwestern, Marquette, and Tulane universities. It had never occurred to her that she might be accepted by all of them. Since she had never ranked her choice of schools, they were all equally desirable to her. Her first thought was to take a few days off from school to visit the five campuses. She suddenly realized that visiting them would mean traveling from her home in Chicago to upstate New York, to Iowa, to California, to Wisconsin, and then to Louisiana. For Kim, this just wasn't feasible. Not only would she have to take several days off from school to fly to five different parts of the country, but she would also have to spend her summer savings for the trips. Kim realized that she had to do some "homework" to eliminate some of the schools from her list. She decided that the best way to do this was to use the College Preference Table (see Figure 9–1).

Figure 9–1 College Preference Table

	Distance	Student Body	Setting	Curriculum	Extra-curricular Activities	Prestige	Housing	Facilities
First Choice College (5 points)	Marquette U.	Drake U.	Southwestern U.	Drake U.	Tulane U.	Tulane U.	Tulane U.	Syracuse
Second Choice College (4 points)	Drake U.	Tulane U.	Drake U.	Tulane U.	Southwestern U.	Marquette U.	Syracuse	Drake U.
Third Choice College (3 points)	Syracuse U.	Southwestern U.	Tulane U.	Marquette U.	Drake U.	Drake U.	Drake U.	Tulane
Fourth Choice College (2 points)	Southwestern U.	Syracuse	Marquette U.	Syracuse U.	Syracuse	Southwestern U.	Marquette U.	Southwestern U.
Fifth Choice College (1 point)	Tulane U.	Marquette U.	Syracuse	Southwestern U.	Marquette U.	Syracuse U.	Southwestern U.	Marquette

Each college that is placed in a first choice position receives five points, and so forth. After tallying up the points for each college, the totals are:

Drake – 31 preference points
Tulane – 30 preference points
Marquette – 21 preference points
Southwestern – 20 preference points
Syracuse – 20 preference points

87

The College Preference Table is a simple chart that helps you rate the many aspects of any university. These concerns can include the school's setting, the variety of courses, the size of the student body, extracurricular activities, or anything else you feel is important. In Kim's case, since there were five schools to consider, she listed them under those concerns that had a bearing on her decision. She ranked the five schools according to the degree to which a particular college met a particular concern. For example, one of Kim's concerns was the distance the college was from her home. She lived in Illinois, and she wanted a school that was within a few hours by car. Of her choices, the ideal place was Marquette, since it was in nearby Wisconsin.

Kim's next concern was to attend a school with an undergraduate student body of about five thousand. The school that came closest to this size was Drake, therefore Drake was her first preference in terms of the size of the student body. Kim continued to list more of her concerns and followed the same procedure for ranking the five schools under each concern.

After completing the College Preference Table, Kim tallied up all of the schools listed and attached a point system for first, second, third, fourth, and fifth choices. Respectively, she gave them five points, four points, three points, two points, and one point. Kim decided that the schools that received the fewest preference points would be dropped from her list. As the chart shows, Drake and Tulane received far more points than the other three colleges. Therefore, Kim was left to decide between the two.

This College Preference Table is one of the best tools for helping you make your decision. By putting everything down on paper, you can see which colleges satisfy your needs and concerns. Naturally, another person's chart would look different from Kim's. First of all, their concerns would be totally different. Second, one person can have the same concerns but interpret them differently. For example, many students believe that distance is a major concern, as Kim did. For Kim, a short distance was a first choice. But for another, a short distance could mean disaster, thereby earning it last place.

Making the Last Visits

An important thing to realize is that Kim was able to eliminate choices without spending money on long plane trips. She simply relied on her college catalogs to give her the factual material she needed. In making the final decision between Drake and Tulane universities, Kim decided that she could afford the trips. She called in advance to the admissions offices to make sure that they could provide a room that she could share for a night with a student. A short phone call eliminated the hassles of staying in a costly hotel or motor inn.

A Situation—Only Accepted by Safety School

If you're like most people, you won't have the worry of getting into too many colleges. You'll most likely have to deal with settling on that safety school that you never really liked. Jimmy had applied to several colleges throughout the country, but he was finally rejected by all except Hamilton College, a small liberal arts school in upstate New York. Although he had applied to Hamilton, it had never occurred to him that he might have to matriculate there. As a native of St. Louis, Missouri, Jimmy had no desire to travel all the way to the East Coast to attend a small college in a hick town.

You may think that Jimmy doesn't have much of a choice in the matter, but actually he has a few choices: (1) he could attend Hamilton for all four years; (2) he could begin school with the hopes of transferring after a year or two (see Rule Three for information on transferring); and (3) he could accept the offer of admission but ask to defer a year. During this period he might want to reapply to those first-choice schools and hope that they take him on the second time around. In many cases the most sensible choice is to try the safety school and attempt a transfer later. This is what Jimmy decided to do.

He remembered that he had chosen Hamilton as a safety because it did not have extremely high standards. He therefore decided that he could probably get a good grade-point average during the first year and get into a good school later.

A Situation—Rejected by Every School

Sounds impossible, doesn't it? Well, believe it or not, it happens all the time. Many students overestimate their high school records and underestimate the college's willingness to reject. Don't feel that the college has a lot to lose if it rejects you. School officials will quickly fill your space. But, on the other hand, don't think you've lost everything simply because you were rejected. There are a lot of ways to get through this situation.

If you have the slightest inkling that you are going to be rejected by some of your colleges, don't tell people where you're applying. If people insist on questioning you, simply tell them that you are considering traveling and enjoying the finer side of life for a year. In other words, make them think *they* are missing out on something too. After all, it's very chic to go abroad to travel during one of your college years. People don't have to know your secrets unless you want to tell them.

So you ask whether there are other ways to deal with your rejections. Fortunately, there are a few strategies, but you've got to be persistent to make them work.

Strategy One

If you're aggressive, you can do what Lynda did. Lynda had been rejected by all the Ivies, but that didn't get her down. She swore that she wouldn't give up until she was in one of her favorite colleges. As soon as Lynda got her rejection letters, she decided to take the bull by the horns and start making phone calls to family friends who had clout (clout doesn't have to mean someone in education—just someone with a big name, a good position, and a nice title). Lynda grabbed hold of a few alumni and had them make a few calls. She also sent out a letter to each admissions officer at each school, explaining her continued interest in their respective schools. She was surprised to see what a network she had created by being aggressive. Of course, this doesn't work for everyone, but Lynda was able to go for a second interview at one of the schools and was then put on the waiting list for that fall. Remember that many colleges won't even talk to you after you've been rejected, even if you nag, plead, complain, or beg. It's a lucky few who can get the admissions people to reverse decisions, but it can be done! As for Lynda, she had nothing to lose.

Strategy Two

If you aren't up to using Lynda's strategy, you may want to do what Eric did. After being rejected by eight colleges, Eric spoke to his high school counselor about his situation. His counselor had strongly recommended Eric and felt an instant concern about the situation (especially after Eric's parents gave the counselor a phone call). Since most counselors have contacts at a few colleges, they can be key figures in the selection process. Eric asked his counselor if she would phone any schools that she had contact with and inform them of his grades, scores, and activities.

In the meantime Eric sent letters to those colleges that his counselor was presently calling. In his letters he enclosed his test scores, grades, and information about his extracurricular activities. Luckily, Eric was just the type that one of the colleges had been looking for. They asked him to fill out an application and then accepted him.

Strategy Three

The next technique is basically a combination of several strategies. After having been rejected by several schools, Blaire refused to take no for an answer. She quickly wrote to the College Acceptance and Admission Service at 516 Fifth Avenue in New York City. This organization is designed to help place students into colleges. The students that seek help from this group are usually those who, for one reason or another, were not accepted by their choice schools. While waiting for an answer, Blaire began to look through a list of colleges that provided an open-enrollment admissions process. These were schools that did not use any selective process for admitting applicants.

Blaire considered applying to a few less competitive colleges; she called a few of them and asked if they would at least consider her application for the second semester. Blaire's next move was to look back over her high school records and figure out why her original list of colleges had rejected her. Since she had great activities and recommendations, she knew that it must have been her grades and scores that kept her out. Realizing this weakness, Blaire planned a semester of night courses in those subjects that gave her problems. She also signed up for an SAT review course, which met once a week. To Blaire, the extra cost of strengthening her weaknesses was worth it. Where is Blaire now? She's a history major in a medium-sized selective university in Texas. Although it wasn't the first choice on her original list, she's happy that she had the determination to keep pushing. You will be too.

Rule Ten:
Following the
No-Procrastination
College Calendar

To be honest, college planning is not one of the most exciting ways to spend your time. If you're in the ninth or tenth grade now, college seems a long way off. If you're a junior or senior or a parent or a college student who wants to transfer, college seems too close for comfort. No matter who you are or where you are in the college process, you have to make some plans. In the next few pages you'll find a calendar that takes you from the beginning of ninth grade to the time when you make your final decision on colleges.

Of course, it's ideal to start at the beginning, but it's up to you to begin where you want. Whether you're too nervous to think about making a schedule for yourself or whether you're just too lazy, it has been done for you *month-by-month for four years*. In addition to following the No-Procrastination College Calendar, you should stay abreast of all that goes on in your school guidance office and ask questions if you don't know what's going on. If you think you missed doing some of the things that the No-Procrastination College Calendar tells you to do, then just try to go back and do them as soon as you can.

No-Procrastination College Calendar

Ninth Grade

September

1. Speak with your guidance counselor and make a list of a tentative group of school courses that you would need to take during the next four years. Make sure it includes all those courses that *your* high school requires of its students. Also follow the recommended course outline in Rule Two when making your plans. Make sure that this year includes a wide selection of courses in each subject.

2. Develop a good working relationship with your new counselor.

October

1. This is a popular month for college fairs. Many schools will give students a day off to visit the college fair in their communities. (A college fair is a gathering of college representatives from all over the country, who set up booths to display and hand out material.) These fairs are good places for speaking to representatives and finding out which colleges are where. Even if you have no questions, take their brochures and catalogs for later use.

2. Investigate your school's extracurricular activities. Now that you're settled into class, you can think about what hobbies or talents you can explore or continue. Join a couple of the school clubs or groups in your community.

November

1. Check around your school to see if there are any upcoming class reunions for recent graduating classes from your school. The Thanksgiving vacation is a great time for get-togethers, where you can mingle with recent high school graduates who are now in college. Ask them questions about their colleges. Don't worry about embarrassing them because all college students love to talk about their schools during these brief vacations with the "old hometown folks."

2. Stop in on your guidance counselor to see if there is any new or important information.

3. Try to develop a good rapport with your teachers by coming for extra help every now and then (even when you don't need help) or to discuss class topics.

December

1. Assess your quality of work. Since it's not yet midyear, decide if you are in need of extra tutoring. Don't let time slip away if you're falling behind.

2. Find out if you need to take any special exams. Many students in New York State are required to take the regents exam. Some of the exams are in January.

3. Enjoy your vacation and keep up with your hobbies or weekend swimming, gymnastics, ice skating, or painting, etc.

4. If you are really behind at school, set aside two full vacation days to catch up, since the marking period probably ends in mid-January.

January

1. If you're starting any new courses for this new semester, make sure they're useful and at the right level of difficulty.

2. This is a good time to stop in at the principal's, or headmaster's, office to tell him you are enjoying the year. This will help you develop a rapport with him. Don't be shy—he'll be impressed by your initiative.

3. It may be time to apply for acceptance into next year's honors or accelerated courses. Ask your counselor about these classes.

February

1. Your school probably has some type of awards assembly each May or June. Now is the time to speak to tenth or eleventh grade friends and ask them what the past awards were and how one is chosen for them. Apply for them, if necessary, since they are good for your future college record.

2. Keep up to date with your guidance counselor to make sure you're kept informed of new information.

March

1. If you are in a half-year course, this is usually the final month to withdraw if you are doing poorly.

2. As the spring season rolls in, so do PTA bake sales. Give a couple hours of your time to them. Urge your parents to give some time too because the PTA carries a lot of weight at high school faculty meetings, and that can make a difference when you want recommendations later.

3. Keep up with your activities, but don't get overinvolved.

April

1. Sit down with your guidance counselor to settle on definite course plans for next year. Keep all requirements in mind.

2. On your own, make any necessary alterations in your long-term high-school course plans.

3. Think about what you want to do this summer. If you want a good job, you had better start early in the month to call employers.

May

1. This is another popular month for college fairs. Collect as much information as possible, and read it when you get a chance.

2. Make final arrangements for next year's courses.

3. Look into summer programs that you may want to be a part of. Music, art, and drama programs for summer weekdays or weekends are great.

4. Since finals are coming up, make sure you understand the work. Get a tutor if necessary.

June

1. Curb your time in extracurricular activities, but don't cut them out completely. You don't want to take up too much time having fun, especially with finals coming up now.

2. Study for finals. Go to extra-help sessions if they are available, and take any required exams, such as the regents if you are a resident of New York State.

3. Stop in at your teachers' and administrators' offices and wish them all a good summer.

4. Ask your counselor if there are any summer events you should know about.

5. Register for summer school if you need to repeat, get ahead of, or brush up on courses.

July

1. Enjoy the summer and your activities. Make an effort to meet the directors of any programs in which you participate. You may want to call on them later in your high school career.

2. If you have a job, be conscientious at your work and make a good impression.

August

1. Before you terminate your summer job, ask your employer for a written recommendation. Tell him you may need it for your college applications. Give him enough notice to write the letter. You want to get it *before* you stop working.

2. A week after you finish your summer activities or jobs, send a thank-you note to the employer or director, telling him of your appreciation for the summer job or program.

3. Think about the courses you'll be taking and ask any students which teachers they would recommend for those classes. Don't wait until you get into a class to find out that your teacher is a lemon.

Tenth Grade

September

1. Start your new classes, and make good first impressions on your teachers. Remember that these are some of the teachers who will be recommending you to colleges.

2. Stop in at your guidance counselor's office to find out about any new information.

October

1. Continue last year's activities, but try to concentrate more involvement in a few of these groups and clubs. If possible, aim for a leadership position in one of your activities or sports.

2. Attend any college fairs that are in your community. Collect information on as many colleges as possible, and ask the college representatives lots of questions. Read through the material on the weekends and during coming vacations.

November

1. Try to talk to college students who recently graduated from your high school. When they're home for the Thanksgiving vacation, they can give you some advice.

2. Spend time on your activities, but keep a balance with your schoolwork.

3. Keep a camera around for any performances or events you participate in during the year. Have a friend take a snapshot of you in the school play or receiving a new award for the Boy Scouts or Girl

Scouts or even playing on the tennis team. These photographs will come in handy for college interviews and applications.

December

1. Make sure your guidance counselor has given you any essential information on college planning or on high school workshops and seminars for the year.

2. Use the vacation to start a speed-reading course. These courses are helpful when the college entrance exams come around. Speed is important on these exams, and a few lessons on speed-reading can aid you later in college.

3. Stop in at the school administrators' office and keep up a good rapport so that they'll remember you later.

January

1. With the new semester, you may want to make sure that you are fulfilling your high school's course requirements for graduating.

2. Look over your long-term high school course plan, and make sure you are on target.

3. Apply for any advanced or accelerated courses for next year if you are interested.

February

1. If you have a winter vacation during this month, use it to volunteer a few days at a local hospital or nursing home. The experience and the feeling of helping others is very rewarding.

2. Think about your high school awards assembly, and decide on how you can line up a way to win some of the awards by the end of the year.

March

1. Ask your guidance counselor about available vocational strength tests. These are brief exams that help identify your talents and tell you which careers are best suited for you. The information is for your use only. No one else sees it, not even the colleges. It's a fun test to take, and it may help you guide your education.

2. Make an extra effort in your classwork by going for extra help and handing work in on time; some high schools ask for teacher evaluations of students.

3. Register for late spring achievement tests.

April

1. Work hard in your school and community activities. Maybe you can send information on any great things you're doing to the educational section of the neighborhood newspaper. You can clip the articles and save them for later.

2. Plan your courses for the eleventh grade, and try to allow room for a typing class. If you can't fit a typing class in, plan one for the summer.

3. Start shopping around for a summer job.

4. Study for your achievement tests. You should take at least one now.

May

1. Stop by your administrators' offices to keep them up to date of your activities and to let them know what fine classes you have.

2. Take your first achievement tests this month. You may take as many as three at one time, but one is probably sufficient. Don't forget that you can cancel the scores at the conclusion of the exam if you don't think the score will be that good.

3. Ask your guidance counselor when the Preliminary Scholastic Aptitude Test (PSAT) will take place. This test helps determine some of the college scholarships you can receive.

June

1. Make sure you have definite plans for the summer. You may want to look into some summer programs at one of the colleges or boarding schools. These programs can give you an idea of what college is like. You'll also have the chance to meet a lot of college-bound students like yourself.

2. Ask some eleventh grade friends about last year's PSAT. Find out if they needed to study for it.

3. Study hard for your finals, and get a tutor if you don't think you'll do well. These grades are very important to colleges.

4. Leave a good last impression on your guidance counselor. Thank him for the assistance given to you.

July

1. During the summer, buy a book to review for the PSAT. You may also want to review some more by looking over last year's math.

2. If you travel during the summer, keep a rough log of your experiences so that you can mention important events in your college essays. Also take photographs of yourself hiking or touring Paris, etc. You want to have photographs that show what you were actually doing in the summer.

3. Speak to college students who are home for the summer and ask them about their schools.

August

1. Take part in any contests or tournaments if you want to win some awards for your hobbies or in sports.

2. Ask your employer if he has any type of college-payment program. In many fields of employment there are programs that give past student employees college scholarships. Also, get a letter of recommendation from your employer before you leave. Leave a good impression on co-workers.

3. Study for the PSAT!

4. Send away for a college application at any two colleges you desire. This will give you an idea of what the applications ask for and how long the forms are. Save them until you begin the real college search.

Eleventh Grade

September

1. Meet with your guidance counselor, and discuss your courses for the current and the senior year.

2. Find out about college-planning sessions at your high school.

3. Study for the PSAT, which will be coming up soon.

4. Develop very good relationships with all your teachers, and renew friendships with former teachers. Keep in touch with the school administrators.

October

1. Take the Preliminary Scholastic Aptitude Test (PSAT).

2. Attend any college fairs that are in your community. Once you've collected all the information from each of the fair's college representatives, read it through. List which schools appeal to you.

3. Start looking through one of those large college catalogs to read about any colleges that come to mind.

November

1. Stay involved in activities, and try to gain leadership positions, if possible. Save any newspaper articles that mention you in any way.

2. Continue to read about the colleges you've heard about. When vacation comes, be prepared to speak to recent high school graduates and to ask them about their colleges. Also ask them if you might visit them for a day or two later in the year.

3. Get hold of a SAT review book, and take a sample test without any practice. If you feel you need help, ask other students about SAT review courses.

December

1. Keep your grades as high as possible. Calculating your grade-point average may scare you into reality and cause you to work harder.

2. Continue to read about various colleges, and use the holidays to speak to college students. Get their impressions on their colleges and find out what mistakes they made while applying.

3. Put a lot into your activities, if you can afford the time.

4. Meet with your guidance counselor to make sure you are taking the best college-bound courses for this semester and next. Also, discuss your counselor's suggestions for college plans.

January

1. You may want to register for a SAT course, if you feel you won't study on your own. If it's too expensive, get some friends together for a study group on a once-a-week basis to review SAT questions.

2. If you want to take a midwinter SAT or ACT, it's now time to register for them.

3. Make a large list of colleges that interest you.

4. Apply for any advanced or accelerated course offered next year.

February

1. If you have the PSAT results, look over your scores and discuss your weaknesses with your guidance counselor.

2. Continue to study for your late spring SAT; you may take your midwinter SAT now, if you registered.

3. Keep up old ties with your old teachers by stopping in at their offices after school. Talk to the administrators, and tell them how much you're enjoying school. Let them know about your school activities.

4. Volunteer for any school functions, such as tour guide at "open houses" for parents.

5. Make sure your parents have met your favorite teachers and all the administrators, since you'll soon be asking them for college recommendations.

March

1. You can register soon for your spring SAT and achievement tests. Start a review program for your exams, if you haven't already.

2. Meet with your counselor to discuss which courses you should take next year and which exams you must take. Also ask your counselor about any special exams you should take to qualify for special scholarships.

3. Check with your bank to find out about special loan programs available to college-bound students.

4. Look deeper into your favorite colleges. Utilize the suggestions of Rule Three, and read any catalogs you come by. Using your list of colleges, write away for more general brochures and information.

April

1. Take the SAT, if you have registered for it. If you are now getting back scores from a previous test, you can figure out a few tentative safety schools for your list. Safety schools should fall well within the range of the SAT score you have received. Your college catalogs give the preferred SAT scores and grade-point averages for particular colleges. These are to be considered as rough estimates, except for the safety schools.

2. Send away for all college applications and information on financial aid.

3. This is the time to sign up for the May achievement tests and the June SAT.

May

1. Call the most popular schools to set up interviews for the summer.

2. Study as much as possible for your SAT and take your achievement tests.

3. All-nighters are most likely to occur this month. If necessary, stay up at night until you finish everything. Don't panic because you've got finals next month.

4. Cut down some of your extracurricular involvement.

5. Look for summer jobs as soon as possible.

6. Attend any college fairs that are in your area.

June

1. Meet with your counselor to confirm next year's courses. Make it an impressive list of courses so that the colleges know you are a naturally studious person.

2. Continue with your activities.

3. Decide on a summer job early in the month because finals are coming up fast.

4. Stop in at the administrators' offices, and tell them how wonderful everything has been for you at their high school.

5. Make your plans to visit the colleges, and set up several interviews for the summer months and for fall of next year.

6. If you haven't taken the SAT yet, take it this month.

July

1. Begin your summer jobs and activities, and ask for more recommendations from directors and employers.

2. Begin organizing your college material in an alphabetical accordion-type folder file. These inexpensive cardboard folders can be carried wherever you need them.

3. Visit the colleges that interest you. Practice for interviews by getting an interview at a school you really don't care about. Also follow the instructions given on interviews in Rule Eight.

August

1. Speak to college students who are home and ask them about the colleges that interest you. They may know something you don't.

2. Begin to fill out some of the application forms, and make a deadline sheet so you have all the necessary dates at your fingertips.

3. Think about the courses you're taking the next semester. Do any necessary reviewing for them, if you want to raise your grade-point average. The first semester of senior year provides your last set of grades to go to the colleges.

4. If you have time, do some volunteer work.

Twelfth Grade

September

1. Meet with your guidance counselor, and make sure you've taken all the right courses and exams. Ask any questions about college that you want your counselor to answer before you mail your completed applications.

2. Keep in mind that you will have to mail your applications by the end of October if you are applying for early decision colleges.

3. Think about those teachers and administrators whom you would like to write your college recommendations. Approach them and follow the instructions in Rule Seven.

4. Study for the November SAT, if you plan to take it.

October

1. Register for the November SAT, if you are still not satisfied with earlier SAT scores. This is basically your last opportunity to take a SAT whose scores will be reported on time for colleges.

2. Attend any college fairs so that you can make sure there are no colleges you haven't thought about.

3. Now you can finish up those college interviews that you couldn't arrange during the summer.

4. Collect recommendations from all activity directors, volunteer organizations, or employers whom you've worked for.

5. Make sure that your counselor knows about the mailing of transcripts and the high school report.

November

1. Make sure that you have forwarded your previous scores from the testing service to all of your colleges.

2. Fill out financial-aid forms with your parents. If the forms are very confusing, get help from your counselor.

3. Try to complete as many applications as possible, since your first-semester course finals are approaching. You don't want to get bogged down in filling out applications during test time.

4. For those of you who want to take the SAT one last time: Some colleges will still accept the scores from next month's exam. Register now for the test and study as much as possible.

December

1. Drop in on those who are writing recommendations for you, and see if they have mailed their letters to your colleges.

2. Take the December SAT, if you registered for it.

3. Look into college scholarship programs offered by organizations. Your parents or relatives may belong to a group that awards annual scholarships. Use a scholarship search group, if you don't have enough luck on your own.

4. Try to score well on all of your finals because these are the last grades that will affect your chances of being accepted by a college.

5. If you applied for an early decision from any college, you should hear sometime this month.

January

1. Send in any last college applications that had late deadline dates.

2. If you feel you will need any help from contacts, use them now. Don't wait until too late to have them write or call.

3. Ask your counselor if it is time to register for advanced placement exams. Although these exams are expensive to register for, getting college credit for high school work will be worth the extra money.

4. Since next year's college tuition bills will be high, you're going to need the highest-paying summer job you can find. Get a jump on everyone by starting to look for a job now. You may want to start an after-school part-time job in order to continue that job through the summer.

February

1. Update all of your college applications by sending information about anything you've done in your activities. Keep your name in the minds of the admissions officers.

2. Keep looking for summer jobs.

3. Keep looking for college scholarships.

4. Relax and have fun.

March

1. Keep up your work so your grade-point average doesn't fall. Although this is senior slump, you can still be rejected by your colleges, and then you'll need a good grade-point average to reapply.

2. In your spare time keep volunteering, and stay with your activities.

3. Continue your summer job search and your financial-aid search.

4. Don't allow yourself to panic about next month's college letters.

April

1. As you receive rejections and acceptances, make your final decisions by the end of the month. If you were completely rejected or can't decide where to go, read Rule Nine.

2. If you were a financial-aid applicant, see what provisions the colleges have made for your financial-aid package.

3. Make your last visits to the colleges, if you still can't decide where to attend.

May

1. Contact the colleges to let them know if you have accepted their offers.

2. You should take the advanced placement exams in any courses for which you want college credit.

3. Make your final search for a summer job that will give you extra spending money for college.

4. Thank your guidance counselor, your parents, and all those who wrote recommendations and gave you assistance during the entire selection process.

Your No-Procrastination College Calendar
Ninth Grade

Sept. _____

_____

Oct. _____

_____

Nov. _____

_____

Dec. _____

_____

Jan. _____

_____

Feb. _____

_____

Mar. _____

_____

Apr. _____

_____

May _____

_____

June _____

_____

July _____

_____

Aug. _____

_____

Your No-Procrastination College Calendar
Tenth Grade

Sept. _____

_____

Oct. _____

_____

Nov. _____

_____

Dec. _____

_____

Jan. _____

_____

Feb. _____

_____

Mar. _____

_____

Apr. _____

_____

May _____

_____

June _____

_____

July _____

_____

Aug. _____

_____

Your No-Procrastination College Calendar
Eleventh Grade

Sept. _____

_____

Oct. _____

_____

Nov. _____

_____

Dec. _____

_____

Jan. _____

_____

Feb. _____

_____

Mar. _____

_____

Apr. _____

_____

May _____

_____

June _____

_____

July _____

_____

Aug. _____

_____

Your No-Procrastination College Calendar
Twelfth Grade

Sept. _____

_____

Oct. _____

_____

Nov. _____

_____

Dec. _____

_____

Jan. _____

_____

Feb. _____

_____

Mar. _____

_____

Apr. _____

_____

May _____

_____

June _____

_____

July _____

_____

Aug. _____

_____

Appendix

Financial Aid

In additon to the information on financial aid from Rule Nine, this appendix can direct you to other sources that can supplement your financial awards or scholarships. The following books can aid you in your search for aid.

Cash for College, Freede, S. Robert. Englewood Cliffs, NJ: Prentice-Hall, 1975.

Financial Aid Guide for College, Suchar, Elizabeth W. New York: Monarch Press, 1978.

Barron's Handbook of American College Financial Aid, Proia, Nicholas C. and DiGaspari, Vincent. Woodbury, NY: Barron's Educational Series, 1978.

Your Own Financial Aid Factory, Leider, Robert. Princeton, NJ: Peterson's Guides, 1980.

How to Get the Money for College, Hawes, Gene R., and Brownstone, David M. NY: David McKay, 1978.

A Guide to Money for College, Scaringi, Louis T. and Joyce W. Bowie, MD: The Anchorage, 1979.

Directory of Financial Aid for Women, Schlachter, Gail Ann. Los Angeles: Reference Service Press, 1978.

The Official College Entrance Examination Board Guide to Financial Aid for Students and Parents, The College Entrance Examination Board, NY: Simon & Schuster, 1980.

Computerized scholarship research services are available for students throughout the country. They provide you with sources of financial assistance if you send them information about your background and future plans. Two of the better-known services are

Scholarship Search
1775 Broadway
New York, NY 10019
(212) 586-5550

National Scholarship Research Service
P.O. Box 2516
San Rafael, CA 94912

More Scholarships and Grants

If you're planning on a career in public service, you can apply for up to $5,000 a year from the Harry S. Truman Scholarship Foundation. Write to:

>Truman Scholarship Foundation
>712 Jackson Place, NW
>Washington, DC 20006

Children of retired, deceased, or disabled parents can receive grants from Social Security. These benefits can be described in detail by your Social Security office.

High school student leaders can apply for the Century III scholarship at the high school guidance office during the school year. Winners can receive more than $10,000.

Whether you are applying for the first time or about to transfer, the Elks Foundation provides over a thousand awards to students. Write to the Elks Foundation in your community for specific requirements.

Each year the Soroptomist Youth Citizenship Awards are given to high school seniors who display promise and leadership. Write to:

>Soroptomist Federation
>1616 Walnut Street
>Philadelphia, PA 19103

Students whose active, retired, or deceased parents have affiliations with the army are eligible for awards and loans from the Department of the Army. Write to:

>Army Emergency Relief
>Department of the Army
>Washington, DC 20314

There is a pamphlet made available by the United Student Aid Funds, Inc., which lists many companies providing student loan programs for children of employees. See if your parent's company is included. Ask for the pamphlet "Low Cost Loans for Education" from:

>United Student Aid Funds, Inc.
>200 E. 42 Street
>New York, NY 10017

If you've got a special hobby or talent, try your skill at competing for an award. Send away for the "Advisory List of National Contests and Activities" from:

>National Association of
>   Secondary School Principals
>1904 Association Drive
>Reston, VA 22091

Scholarships Awarded by Religious Groups

Information on scholarships that are based on religious affiliation can be received by writing to:

American Baptist Student Aid Fund
Board of Education Ministries
Valley Forge, PA 19481

Catholic Aid Association
49 West Ninth Street
St. Paul, MN 55102

Student Grants and Loans
Personnel Services
Jewish Welfare Board
15 East 26 Street
New York, NY 10010

Aid Association for Lutherans
Educational Benevolences
Appleton, WI 54919

Student Scholarships
The United Methodist Church
Board of Higher Education and Ministry
P.O. Box 871
Nashville, TN 37202

National Presbyterian
United Presbyterian Church in the USA
475 Riverside Drive, Room 430
New York, NY 10027

If you're a minority member and are sports oriented, there is help for college funding. Write to:

Lee Elder Scholarship Fund
1725 K Street, NW
Washington, DC 20006

There's another foundation that supplies grants to minority freshmen or other students who plan to major in business, engineering, pre-law, pre-med, math sciences, or pre-dentistry. Write to:

George E. Johnson Foundation
8522 South Lafayette Avenue
Chicago, IL 60620

Scholarships are available to female students if they send away for the pamphlet "Educational Financial Aid Sources for Women" by writing to:

Clairol Loving Care Scholarship Program
345 Park Avenue, 5th floor
New York, NY 10022

Another listing of scholarships is called "Financial Aid: A Partial List of Resources for Women." Write to:

Project on the Status and Education of Women
Association of American Colleges
1818 R Street, NW
Washington, DC 20009

The General Motors Corporation offers four-year college scholarships to high school seniors. To find out which colleges participate in this program, write to:

General Motors Scholarship Program
8-163 GM Building
Detroit, MI 48202

Four-year scholarships which pay for full tuition are available to high school students through the Proctor and Gamble Company. Write to:

Proctor and Gamble Scholarships
M.A. and R. Building
Ivorydale, OH

High school students who are interested in science, math, or engineering are eligible for the Westinghouse Science Talent Award. For information, write to:

Science Clubs of America
1719 N Street, NW
Washington, DC 20036

Sample Forms

FLAXMAN HIGH SCHOOL
Flaxman, Oregon
STUDENT AWARDS AND ACTIVITY RECORD

Mr.
Miss _____
    (Last Name)   (First Name)   (Middle)   (Address)

	GRADE 9	GRADE 10	GRADE 11	GRADE 12
	19	19	19	19
AWARDS AND HONORS				
Jr. Nat. Honor Society				
Sr. Nat. Honor Society				
RECOGNITION				
For Scholarship				
For Service				
For Athletics				
STUDENT GOVERNMENT				
Committee Chairman				
Committee Member				
Boys' State				
Girls' State				

	GRADE 9	GRADE 10	GRADE 11	GRADE 12
	19	19	19	19
PUBLICATIONS				
Newspaper				
Yearbook				
Literary Magazine				
G.O. Newsletter				
ATHLETICS				
Baseball — Varsity				
Basketball — Varsity				
Basketball — JV				
Basketball — Intramural				

Cross Country						
Football – Varsity						
Football – Jr. Varsity						
Golf						
Gymnastics						
Softball						
Swimming						
Tennis						
Track CC, I, O						
Volleyball						
Cheerleader						
Ice Hockey Varsity						
Ice Hockey JV						

PERFORMING ARTS

Dramatics						
Band						
Choir (A Capella)						
Orchestra						
String Ensemble						
Wind Ensemble						
Brass Sextet						
Glee Club						

ELECTED OFFICES

LaCrosse						
Soccer – Varsity						
Soccer – JV						
Wrestling – Varsity & JV						
Field Hockey						
Marching Corps (Color)						
Guard, Tigerettes, Bengalettes						

Gen'l Organization						
Legislature						
G.O. Officer						
Class						
House						

_____ PRINCIPAL _____

DATE _____

Wesleyan University

MIDDLETOWN, CONNECTICUT 06457

Admissions Information Form

1

F 33

This form is a required part of the application process. As soon as you have decided to apply to Wesleyan we encourage you to complete this form and send it to Wesleyan, with the $30. application fee and Application Voucher (Form 2). This will enable us to set up your application file as early as possible so we can begin compiling all materials which support your application. You may take more time to complete your essays, submitting them in accordance with the deadline of the admissions program you have selected. We are aware that some questions asked below duplicate those you have answered elsewhere in the application materials. However, this form serves a dual purpose; it provides the basis for student records maintained by the Registrar's office should you matriculate at Wesleyan and it provides comprehensive historical and statistical data on the class entering in 1981. **Please follow instructions carefully, and use a ballpoint pen. Print carefully using capital letters only, one letter (or digit) per space. Use codes listed on the reverse side of this form where indicated. Do not write in gray boxes.**

Social Security No: ___-___-___
1

Name: _____
10 LAST

22 FIRST

32 MIDDLE INITIAL 35

Admissions Program
R - Regular Decision
1 - Early Decision Option I
2 - Early Decision Option II
M - Mid-Year Enrollment
34

Plan to Enter (F-Fall Semester; S-Spring Semester):

Telephone Number (through June 15):
36 AREA CODE

High School Name: _____

High School Type: (P-Public; I-Independent; C-Parochial): 52

Date of Graduation:
(in numbers)

[ ] [ ]
53 MONTH

[ ] [ ]
55 YEAR

Academic Interest:
(code-see reverse side)

[ ] [ ]
57 1ST CHOICE

[ ] [ ]
59 2ND CHOICE

[ ]
61 80

1

Mailing Address for Admissions Correspondence (code for name of state-see reverse side):

14 _____
NUMBER AND STREET

36 _____
CITY

[ ] [ ]
58 STATE

[ ] [ ] [ ] [ ] [ ]
60 ZIP

[ ] [ ]
65
RESIDENT STATE
(IF DIFF FROM 58)

Miscellaneous Information:

Did you apply to Wesleyan previously? If yes, enter R:

[ ]
67

Citizenship (code-see reverse side):

[ ]
68

Month/Year of Previous Application: _____

Ethnic Background (code-see reverse side):

[ ]
69

Financial Aid:

Are you applying for financial aid? If yes enter F:

[ ]
70

Sex (M-Male; F-Female):

[ ]
71

Alumni affiliation (if parent or grandparent attended
Wesleyan, enter W):

[ ]
72

Date of Birth:

[ ] [ ]
MONTH
73

[ ] [ ]
DAY

[ ] [ ]
YEAR

Optional Cards - (If you submitted any, enter:)

Name, class, and relationship to you of close
relatives who have attended Wesleyan:

_____

_____

P-Performing Arts Interest
A-Athletic Interest
S-Science Interest

[ ]
79 80

2

Wesleyan University

MIDDLETOWN, CONNECTICUT 06457

Application for Freshman Admission

3

Please type or print

BIOGRAPHICAL INFORMATION

Legal name: _____ _____ _____ _____ Sex: M ___ F ___
Last   First   Middle   Jr., Etc.

Usually called: _____ (nickname)   Former last name(s) if any: _____

Permanent home address: _____
Number and Street

_____ _____ _____
City or town   State   Zip

Permanent home telephone: _____ / _____
Area Code   Number

If different from above, please give your mailing address for all admission correspondence:

Mailing address: _____
Number and Street

_____ _____ _____
City or town   State   Zip

FAMILY

Father's full name: _____   Is he living? _____

(Describe briefly)

Name of college (if any): _____ Degree _____ Year _____

Name of professional or graduate school (if any): _____ Degree _____ Year _____

Mother's full name: _____ Is she living? _____

Home address if different from yours: _____

Occupation: _____ Employer: _____

(Describe briefly)

Name of college (if any): _____ Degree _____ Year _____

Name of professional or graduate school (if any): _____ Degree _____ Year _____

If not with both parents, with whom do you make your permanent home: _____

Please give the names and ages of your brothers or sisters. If they have attended college, give the names of the institutions attended, degrees and approximate dates.

_____

_____

EARLY DECISION STATEMENT

After carefully considering my college applications, I have decided that Wesleyan is my first choice and request an Early Decision on my application. If accepted under the Early Decision Program, I agree to accept the offer of admission and will withdraw all other college applications and initiate no new applications. I am applying for Early Decision under (please check one) Option I _____ (deadline November 15, notification December 15), Option II _____ (deadline January 15, notification February 15)

_____
Your Signature

_____
Name (printed)

(over, please)

EDUCATION

Please list all the secondary schools, including summer schools, programs, and institutes, you have attended, grades 9-12.

Schools attended, present school first

Name of School	Location (City, State, Zip)	Dates attended

Please list all colleges at which you have taken courses for credit and list names of courses on a separate sheet. *Please send a transcript from each institution as soon as possible.*

Name of College	Location (City, state, zip)	Degree Candidate?	Dates attended

If you are not attending school at the present time, please describe what you are doing:

Will you be a candidate for financial aid? Yes _____ No _____

The appropriate College Scholarship Service form was/will be filed on _____ (Date)

_____ of academic concentration:

TEST INFORMATION

Wesleyan requires either the College Entrance Examination Board's Scholastic Aptitude Test (SAT) and Three Achievement Tests (ACH), one of which must be English Composition, or the American College Test (ACT). Please list your test plans below and arrange to have official reports of the tests forwarded to Wesleyan from the College Board.

	(SAT)	(ACH)	Subjects	(ACT)
Dates taken or				
to be taken				

WESLEYAN INTEREST:

How did you become interested in Wesleyan? Indicate significant sources of information or opinion by *underlining* those to which you have been exposed and placing an asterisk (*) beside the most influential.

College handbook or guide   Campus visit   Teacher or parent
College counselor   Saturday panel   Wesleyan alumnus or student
College Night or fair   Interview   Wesleyan publications
                    School visit by Admissions Representative

List any persons who stimulated your interest in Wesleyan, giving their name and relationship to you:

For which reasons did you include Wesleyan among your college choices?

ACADEMIC HONORS

Briefly describe any scholastic distinctions or honors you have won since the ninth grade.

_____

_____

_____

_____

EXTRACURRICULAR AND PERSONAL ACTIVITIES

Please list your principal extracurricular, community and family activities, and hobbies *in order of their interest to you.* For example, musical instrument played, varsity letters earned, special skills, offices held, etc.

Activity	Grade level or year of participation 9 10 11 12	Approximate number of hours spent per week	Positions held honors won

WORK EXPERIENCE

Please list any job (including summer employment) you have held during the past three years.

Specific nature of work	Employer	Approx. dates of employment	Hours per week

PERSONAL STATEMENT

1. It is our aim to get to know you as well as possible through this application. With this in mind, please describe in detail some special interest, experience, or achievement or anything else you would like us to know about you. Essays on a personal, local or national issue that are of particular concern to you are also welcome. Attach extra pages (same size please), if your statement exceeds these limits.

2. Evaluate yourself as a student in terms of your intellectual interests, motivations and aspirations. The Admissions Committee is interested in how you will use Wesleyan's resources for learning and opportunities to direct your education.

My signature below indicates that all the information contained in my application is factually correct and honestly presented.

Signature _____   Date: _____

Confidential

Wesleyan University

FINANCIAL AID APPLICATION

Check one: ☐ Early Decision ☐ Regular Decision
☐ Midyear Admission

(Please Print)

Applicant's
Name _____
Home
Address _____   Birth
                                        Date _____

Phone Number _____

Social Security Number _____

Return to: Director of Financial Aid
Wesleyan University
Middletown, Connecticut 06457

All financial aid offered by Wesleyan is awarded exclusively on the basis of need. The Scholarship Committee endeavors to meet the financial need of every student to whom admission is offered. Because all awards are based on financial need, it is essential that the information requested on this form AND on the Financial Aid Form of the College Scholarship Service be submitted as soon as possible and in no case later than February 1 for freshman and March 1 for transfer applications. We cannot award financial aid unless these forms are completed and returned. All information submitted on these forms will be regarded with absolute confidence and will be used only for the purposes of awarding financial aid.

Note: Wesleyan Financial Aid applicants residing in those states which offer state-funded college grant programs are **required** to file for those grants. Failure to apply for state grants for which you are eligible may result in the loss of your Wesleyan Scholarship. *Your school guidance office will have information on any programs offered by your state.*

Father's Name		Mother's name	
(or spouse)	Age	*(or spouse)*	Age
Address _____		Address _____	
Occupation _____		Occupation _____	
Employer _____	No. of Yrs. _____	Employer _____	No. of Yrs. _____

PARENTS	1 ☐ FATHER 3 ☐ STEPFATHER	Check any 5 ☐ PARENTS SEPARATED * 7 ☐ STUDENT HAS LEGAL GUARDIAN 9 ☐ STUDENT INDEPENDENT	If other unusual family circum-
Check if living:	2 ☐ MOTHER 4 ☐ STEPMOTHER	*that apply:* 6 ☐ PARENTS DIVORCED * 8 ☐ FATHER UNABLE TO WORK (other than parents) 10 ☐ STUDENT MARRIED	stances exist, attach explanation

TO BE COMPLETED BY PARENTS OR INDEPENDENT STUDENT

(ENTER INFORMATION IN BOXES)

	EST. 1980	EST. 1981
1. SALARIES AND WAGES BEFORE TAXES		
A. FATHER, STEPFATHER, GUARDIAN (or Independent Student)	$	$
B. MOTHER, STEPMOTHER, GUARDIAN (or Independent Student's Spouse)	$	$
2. IF SELF-EMPLOYED—BUSINESS INCOME	$	$
3. OTHER INCOME—SPECIFY SOURCE (S.S., V.A., CHILD SUPPORT, ALIMONY, GIFTS)	$	$
SUBTOTAL A: ADD 1A, 1B, 2, and 3	$	$
4. BUSINESS EXPENSES	$	$
4a. TOTAL FEDERAL INCOME TAX PAID	$	$
5. ANNUAL RENT OR MORTGAGE PAYMENTS ON FAMILY RESIDENCE	$	$
6. COST OF ANNUAL MEDICAL INSURANCE PREMIUMS PLUS MEDICAL AND DENTAL EXPENSES NOT COVERED BY INSURANCE	$	$

(ENTER INFORMATION IN BOXES)

		EST. 1980	EST. 1981
7. TOTAL INDEBTEDNESS—(DO NOT INCLUDE CAR, APPLIANCES, FURNITURE)		$	$
	TOTAL FIRE INSURANCE	PRESENT MARKET VALUE	UNPAID MORTGAGE
8. HOME (IF OWNED) YEAR PURCHASED 19 ___ PURCHASE PRICE $ ___	$	$	$
9. OTHER REAL ESTATE	$	$	$
10. BANK ACCOUNTS (TOTAL OF PARENTS' SAVINGS AND CHECKING)			$
11. OTHER INVESTMENTS (PRESENT MARKET VALUE)			$
12. LIST FAMILY CARS OWNED (MAKE & YEARS)			$
TOTAL CAR DEBT			$

*DATE OF DIVORCE OR SEPARATION _____

A NAME OF CHILD OR DEPENDENT	B AGE	C. Check if living with family	D. NAME OF PRESENT SCHOOL OR COLLEGE 1980-81	E. YEAR IN SCHOOL OR COLLEGE 1980-81	EDUCATIONAL EXPENSES IN 1980-81 F. TUITION AND FEES	G. ROOM AND BOARD	FINANCIAL AID RECEIVED IN 1980-81 H. SCHOLAR- SHIPS OR GIFT AID	I. LOANS AND EMPLOYMENT	J. NAME OF INSTITUTION TO BE ATTENDED IN 1981-82	K. Check appropriate boxes) (if attending in 1980-81 Public School	Private School	College	Check If Full- Time Student
Provide below information for ALL CHILDREN and OTHER DEPENDENTS: Do Not leave blank.					$	$	$	$					
1 Student Applicant													
2													
3													
4													
5													
6													

IF STUDENT LIVES WITH: MOTHER ONLY ☐ FATHER ONLY ☐ OTHER ☐ Complete the following:

Name _____

Age _____ Support from other parent $ _____ Relationship to student _____

Type of job _____ Take home pay $ _____

weekly _____
every 2 wks. _____
monthly _____

Date Parents' Financial Aid Form submitted to C.S.S. _____ Wesleyan's code: 3959

I certify that this application has been completed in good faith and without reservations and that I will notify the Director of Financial Aid if there are any significant changes in my financial resources (including other scholarship awards) after this application has been submitted.

Date _____ Signature _____

PARENT

Date _____ Signature _____

STUDENT APPLICANT

If you wish to make any additions or note any unusual circumstances, please do so on additional sheets.

Return to: DIRECTOR OF FINANCIAL AID
WESLEYAN UNIVERSITY
MIDDLETOWN, CT. 06457

Bibliography

On Colleges

Barron's College Profiles In-Depth Series
Woodbury, N.Y.: Barron's Educational Series, various dates.
These are in-depth reports on individual colleges, only available for certain colleges.

Barron's Profiles of American Colleges 2 vols.
Woodbury, N.Y.: Barron's Educational Series, 1980.
These are two catalogs, over a thousand pages of general information on each U.S. college; gives information on tuition, courses offered, housing, etc.

Peterson's Travel Guide to Colleges
Cahill, Matthew, ed. Princeton, N.J.: Peterson's/Hammond Publication, 1977.

Comparative Guide to American Colleges
Cass, James and Birnbaum, Max. New York: Harper & Row, 1979

Comparative Guide to Junior and Two-Year Community Colleges
Cass, James and Birnbaum, Max. New York: Harper & Row, 1972.

The College Blue Book
New York: MacMillan Publishing Company, 1975.

The College Handbook
New York: College Entrance Information Board, 1979.
Information on about three thousand colleges, includes data on requirements, tuition, housing, etc.

College Knowledge
Edelhart, Michael. New York: Doubleday Inc., 1979.

Guide to Alternative Colleges and Universities
Boston: Beacon Press, 1974.

Hawes Comprehensive Guide to Colleges
Hawes, Gene R. New York: New American Library, 1978.

Junior College Directory
Washington, D.C.: American Association of Junior Colleges.

Lovejoy's College Guide
Lovejoy, Clarence E. New York: Simon & Schuster, 1979.
General information for over three thousand U.S. colleges.

Barron's Handbook of College Transfer Information
Proia, Nicholas C. Woodbury, N.Y.: Barron's Educational Series, 1975.
Gives specific transfer information on over a thousand colleges.

Black Colleges in America
Willie, Charles V. and Edwards, Ronald R. New York: Columbia
Teachers College Press, 1978.

The Insider's Guide to the Colleges
Staff of the Yale Daily News.
Information about specific U.S. colleges, prepared by each campus's
own college students.

On Exams

How to Prepare for the Advanced Placement Examinations
Woodbury, N.Y.: Barron's Educational Series, updated yearly.
A different workbook for each exam.

How to Prepare for College Board Achievement Tests Series
Woodbury, N.Y.: Barron's Educational Series, updated yearly.
A different workbook for each exam.

How to Prepare for College Entrance Examinations
Brownstein, Samuel C. and Weiner, Mitchel. Woodbury, N.Y.: Barron's
Educational Series, updated yearly.
Shows how to review for the SAT.

How to Prepare for the PSAT-NMSQT
Brownstein, Samuel C. and Weiner, Mitchel. Woodbury, NY.: Barron's
Educational Series, updated yearly.
NMSQT stands for the National Merit Scholarship Qualifying Test.

Verbal Workbook for the SAT
Freedman, Gabriel P. and Haller, Margaret A. New York: Arco
Publishing Co., 1980.

ACT—Exam Series
Warner, David. New York: Arco Publishing Co., 1977.

About the Author

Lawrence O. Graham, a sophomore at Princeton University, recently went through the college admissions process. He can tell you how to succeed with today's plan for college acceptance. He has been on radio and televison talk shows, including the *Today Show*, and he has been quoted in many national publications, including *Seventeen* Magazine and *The New York Times*. He has given advice to parents and students on the college admissions process in group, as well as individual settings, and at Princeton Career Services, he counsels students on college and career related matters. He has been a producer with WNBC radio and last summer served as an aide for the Assistant to the President in The White House.

If you or your organization, library, or school wish to contact Lawrence Graham—or if you have questions or comments, write:

Lawrence Graham
P.O. Box 1278
Princeton, NJ 08540

Order your NO-PROCRASTINATION COLLEGE CALENDAR POSTER now! 19" x 25", folds to loose-leaf notebook size. Carry wherever you go. Tells the high school student what to do month by month to prepare for college admission. Send $5.00 check to above address.